W9-CHZ-396

Studying Business

The Bridge to Your Future

By
Samuel S. Gaglio
College of Business Administration
University of Notre Dame

Published by:
Discovery Press
Burbank, California

Permissions and Copyrights

Cover design by Dave McNutt.

Adapted from *Studying Engineering: A Road Map to a Rewarding Career*.
Copyright © 1995 by Raymond B. Landis. Used by permission of the author.

Material in Chapter 3 from THE SIX PILLARS OF SELF-ESTEEM by Nathaniel
Branden. Copyright © 1994 by Nathaniel Branden. Used by permission of
Bantam Books, a division of Bantam Doubleday Dell Publishing Group, Inc.

Franklin Chang-Diaz photo in Chapter 2 courtesy of National Aeronautics and
Space Administration.

Studying Business: The Bridge to Your Future

Discovery Press/February, 1999

10 9 8 7 6 5 4 3 2 1

All rights reserved.

Copyright © 1999 by Discovery Press

No part of this book may be reproduced or transmitted in any form or by any means,
electronic or mechanical, including photocopying, recording or by any information
storage and retrieval system, without permission in writing from the author.

Library of Congress Catalog Card Number: 99-70550

ISBN 0-9646969-4-0

Inquiries and comments should be addressed to:

Samuel S. Gaglio, Assistant Dean
College of Business Administration
University of Notre Dame
Notre Dame, IN 46556
Telephone: (219) 631-6602
E-mail: Samuel.s.Gaglio.1@nd.edu

Distributed by:

Legal Books Distributing
4247 Whiteside Street
Los Angeles, CA 90063
Telephone: (213) 526-7110
        (800) 200-7110 (Outside L.A. County)
FAX: (213) 526-7112

Books may be ordered by mail, telephone, or FAX.

To Gayle

TABLE OF CONTENTS

Chapter 3. Personal Development

PREFACE

Congratulations! The fact that you are reading this book means you are going to college and a business degree is your goal. It also means you recognize the need to prepare yourself for a major lifestyle change. Accomplishing any goal in life requires motivation.

I want to share with you my philosophy on life, which has motivated me to accomplish the goals I have set for myself. The process of successful business study can be compared to the process of a successful life. I have lived my life to this point based on a simple three-letter acronym: **LIP.**

LIP stands for **Luck**, **Information** and **Power**—three words which I have used to help understand why I do things, why my goals are important to me and what my goals have to do with my life.

Luck is most often defined as chance or maybe fate. The definition implies that you have no real control over the outcome. My definition of luck has no relationship to chance. Luck is being prepared for an opportunity before you even know it exists. Since you are reading this book, you are most likely a current college student or at least thinking of going to college. You have arrived at a point in your life where you have decided business study is important. You did not arrive at this point by chance, although I am quite confident someone has already said "you are lucky to be in college" or "you are lucky your grade point average (GPA) is high enough to allow you a choice of majors," or some similar comment. You have worked hard for this opportunity from the time you were in grade school. Think of the times you have stayed up to finish a project, read an extra book or studied a little longer for a test. You were creating a personal portfolio which would open doors for future undefined opportunities. In the future, if someone tells you that you are lucky, and they mean you have worked hard for the opportunity, thank them for recognizing your efforts—if they mean chance, then correct them.

Information is knowledge—the ability to know what to do in a situation, how to answer a question, or solve a problem. Today's world is run on information. We read the newspaper, listen to the news, talk to our lawyers, and consult with our doctors. Society is no longer dependent on the strongest person or the best looking person or the person from the "right" family background. The reason you are going to school is to gain information in order to be an information holder. Your success in life will be dependent on the extent to which you know information.

Power is the ability to influence people to accomplish a task. The reason you are in school today is to gain a sense of power. Maybe want to create a revolutionary new product, or you want to be the director of production management for a large firm, or you want to be a stockbroker. No matter what your goal is, you will need power to accomplish that goal. Power is a good thing; the more power you acquire the more you can affect your life and the lives of others. Power used for the good of society is a wonderful tool. Be proud of the fact you are seeking power. Take every opportunity to acquire it and use this power to make this world a better place for all of us.

The basic premise of this book is that a small amount of preparation on your part will lead to an enormous payoff throughout the remainder of your college experience.

Chapter 1 lays the foundation for the entire book by developing three keys for success: 1) determination; 2) effort; and 3) approach. The keys to success are followed by four models, which can help you to understand what is meant by a quality education and how to go about getting that education.

Chapter 2 introduces you to those strategies and approaches that are essential to academic success. Strategies for identifying and utilizing critical resources including peers, professors and other campus professionals. The last section of the chapter is devoted to developing your study skills.

Chapter 3 addresses the subject of personal development. A success model is presented to aid you in understanding the process of and difference between making behavioral and attitudinal adjustments. The concept of change is introduced as a natural process made possible by three catalysts: 1) knowledge; 2) commitment; and 3) action. A section on self analysis will assist you in understanding yourself as well as others. Important personal development topics of assessment, communication skills, and health and wellness are also included in this chapter.

Chapter 4 identifies four extracurricular activities that can greatly improve the quality of your education: 1) student organizations; 2) extracurricular projects; 3) pre-professional employment; and 4) service to the university.

Chapter 5 focuses on the subject of professional development. The primary purpose of the chapter is to motivate you to succeed through an understanding of the business profession and an increased awareness of the rewards and opportunities that will come to you if you graduate in business.

Chapter 6 provides an orientation to the business education system including the accreditation process, the advising system, academic regulations and student ethics. Opportunities for graduate study in business and other disciplines as well as the role of research are also discussed in this chapter.

This book is ideally suited for use in an "Introduction to Business" course. First year students often enter higher education with little or no knowledge about how to be successful at the college level. The basics provided in this book can aid students in developing a framework for academic success. However, the book could be used in a variety of other ways. College sophomores, juniors and even seniors could use the book to help them decide on a college, improve study habits, conduct self assessment, and explore career options. High school students and their parents can read the book prior to making a decision on a university. Business faculty can turn to this book as a resource for both formal and informal advising. University admission officers could use this book in developing recruiting presentations.

Many people have contributed directly or indirectly to the creation of this book in its current form. First and foremost, I owe a debt of gratitude to Ray Landis for encouraging me to write this book and permitting me to adapt his book *'Studying Engineering: A Road Map to a Rewarding Career'*. Thanks also to Martin Roden for his encouragement and advice.

Thanks also to the many individuals who read the early drafts of the book and provided valuable contributions. Included in this group are the three students from Beta Gamma Sigma who unselfishly gave of their time to read the first draft: Cindy Harding, Kimberly Smith and Jeffrey Wawok.

Lastly I would like to acknowledge my wife, Gayle Gaglio, who encouraged me from the very beginning. She shielded me from distractions and designed my home office space where most of this book was developed.

Samuel S. Gaglio
Granger, Indiana

Chapter 1
KEYS TO SUCCESSFUL BUSINESS STUDY

Introduction

I remember my first day as a college freshman very vividly. I was enrolled in a small Midwest business and engineering school attending the first session of my "Introduction to College" course. The dean of students welcomed us to the college with the following statement:

> **Look to your right. Look to your left. Two out of three of you won't be here at graduation.**

It doesn't surprise me that deans (and professors) say such upsetting things to students. They think you will benefit from this message. They think that by scaring you about how difficult and demanding college is, you will be more likely to succeed.

What does surprise me, however, is that I was not provided with a positive message as well as that negative message (the threat of failure). I'm still a little upset that the dean tried to frighten me at a time when I was unsure of myself and easily intimidated.

When I meet with incoming students I try to convey a very different message. My message to them and to you is:

> **Each and every one of you can be successful in graduating with your bachelor's degree in business.**

How can I make such a bold statement without any specific information about you, your background or your ability? Because you will receive that positive message.

The ideas introduced in this chapter will provide a foundation for the remainder of this text. First, I will discuss the three most important traits that will lead you to success in business study:

1

Determination
Effort
Approach

Next, I will present four models from which to view your education. **These models will help you answer important academic and career questions.**

AACSB Model
One Academic Model
Employment Model
Student Involvement Model

1.1 Determination

Of the three traits, the most important is ***determination***. The dictionary defines *determination* as "a firmness of purpose . . . having one's mind made up." Determination means having an unwavering commitment to your goal—the goal of graduating. You must be determined to persist even in the face of adversity.

Former Notre Dame football coach Lou Holtz, a highly sought after motivational speaker, relates a primary difference between people who succeed and people who fail. According to Holtz: "People who succeed are people who when they get 'knocked down' by some adversity, they get up; whereas, people who fail are people who, when they get knocked down, they stay down."

The most likely reason you will fail to graduate is that you will encounter some adversity and give up. You will have difficulty with a course, a fellow student, an administrator, or a professor. Or you will have a personal problem, a relationship problem, or a health problem. You will encounter some adversity and use it as a reason (an "excuse") for quitting.

The Importance of Goal Setting

We'll talk more about the importance of goal setting in a later section. The basic idea behind goal setting is:

> **How can you ever expect to get some where if you don't know where you want to go?**

Start by making graduating in business your primary life goal. Adopt the view that you are going to achieve that goal and that nothing is going to stop you.

Setting goals is the easy part. **Making the goal really important is the real challenge.** By "really important," I mean that you make all of your day-to-day decisions and choices based on whether a particular action supports your goal (moves you closer to your goal) or conflicts with your goal (moves you farther away from your goal).

And how do you keep adversity from stopping you? How can you keep failures from discouraging you? I find the age-old saying

We learn more from our failures
then we do from our successes

to be very helpful as a philosophical basis for overcoming adversity. It's true! Think about it.

Personal Story

> *Early in my career I was working at the regional headquarters of a large business. Even though I was one of the junior-most professionals in the office, one day a senior executive asked me to fill in for him and make a briefing to upper level management. I felt I could handle the job, particularly since the senior executive had already prepared the presentation including necessary visuals, and I accepted the responsibility confidently. Needless to say, it did not go well. Right in the middle of my presentation, the senior management officer present said "If you don't know more about the topic than I do, do not attempt to brief me!" and stormed out of the conference room. I have never been so embarrassed in my life. I learned a tremendous lesson from that experience. Since then, I have never and will never be unprepared for a presentation.*

Learning to Overcome Adversity

Learning to overcome adversity as a student will also benefit you during your professional career. Joseph J. Jacobs, founder and CEO of Jacobs Engineering, and one of the nation's most successful businessmen, gives his "Nine Commandments for the Entrepreneur." The first four are:

1.   **You must be willing to risk failure.**

2.   **You must passionately hate failure.**

3.   **Persistence is a necessity, just as is the willingness to acknowledge defeat and to move on.**

4.   **A measure of your potential to succeed is how you handle adversity.**

I would encourage you to read Mr. Jacob's highly motivational autobiography, *The Anatomy of an Entrepreneur* [1].

If you are determined to graduate in business, if you persist even in the face of adversity, if you take the view that you will not allow anything to stop you, the chances are very good that you will succeed.

> **Believe in yourself. You can do it!**

1.2 Effort

Do you believe that **people succeed because of their ability**—that some people have it and other people don't? Or, do you believe that **people succeed because of their effort**?

The first belief—that some people have it and some don't—is a self-defeating belief. It can provide you with a rationale to accept failure in yourself. If you decide you don't have as much ability as others, you may as well give up. After all, if success is related to some natural quality that you have no control over, then it doesn't matter what you do.

The second belief—that people succeed because of their effort—is empowering, because the amount of effort you put in is in your direct control. You can choose to put in more effort and in doing so directly affect your success.

Effort Defines and Enhances Ability

The relative importance of ability and effort was perhaps best put by the famous American inventor Thomas Edison:

> ### _Genius is one percent inspiration and ninety-nine percent perspiration._

Does the following dialogue sound familiar to you? Over the years I have heard many, many variations of it from my students.

Gaglio:	How's everything going?
Student:	_Fine._
Gaglio:	What is your hardest course?
Student:	_Accounting._
Gaglio:	How are you doing in the course.
Student:	_Ok, I guess._
Gaglio:	What grade did you get on the last exam?
Student:	_I don't know. I haven't picked it up yet._
Gaglio:	Do you think it's an "A"?
Student:	_No._
Gaglio:	Is it a "B"?
Student:	_No._
Gaglio:	Is it a "C"?
Student:	_Yeah. It could be a "C"_
Gaglio:	Have you missed any class sessions this term?
Student:	_Only a few._
Gaglio:	What percentage would you estimate.
Student:	_Twenty-five percent._
Gaglio:	Have you turned in the required homework assignments.
Student:	_Most of them._
Gaglio:	What percentage would you estimate.
Student:	_Eighty percent._
Gaglio:	When is your next exam?
Student:	_Tomorrow._

Gaglio: Are you ready for the exam?

Student: *I expect to be. I plan to cut my Marketing class tomorrow so I can study Accounting.*

Gaglio: Let's finish our discussion about Accounting and then we'll talk about Marketing.

This scenario describes a student who is not putting in appropriate effort and is headed toward failure in one or more courses!

Effort is Both Time and Energy

In my experience, poor academic performance can usually be traced to insufficient effort. Webster's Dictionary defines *effort* as: "the using of energy to get something done; exertion of . . . mental power."

There are two distinct components to the effort you devote to your studies—time and energy. An analogy can be made using the well-known formula:

$$\boxed{\textbf{Distance = Rate x Time}}$$

Completing a specific task (i.e., traveling a distance) requires that you devote energy or mental power (rate) and spend time on the task (time). In the next chapter, we will consider how much time is sufficient, what is the best use of that time, and when to put in that time if you want to be both effective and efficient.

The important point here is that your success in the study of business is to a great extent **in your control**. How well you perform will depend, in large measure, on how much effort you put forth. Accomplishing an academic task, like completing a homework assignment, will require you to devote adequate time and to focus your energy and mental power. These are things that you can choose to do or choose not to do.

1.3 Approach

The approach you take to the study of business will also be a key factor in your success. Although some tasks will depend solely on effort, your effectiveness in accomplishing most tasks will depend on both effort _and_ approach. Even for tasks that depend primarily on effort, it is important that you learn to be efficient in what you do. Otherwise you will waste time unnecessarily and be limited in what you can accomplish. In other words, success in business study requires not only that you work harder, but also **that you work "smarter."**

Becoming a Master Student

If you were to take up chess, what would you do? Learn the basic objectives, rules, and moves and then begin to play? Probably, but you'd soon discover that mastering a game of skill like chess requires much more. So you might read a book, take a lesson, or watch experts play. You would realize that to become a chess _master_, you need to spend time both playing the game and learning about it.

The study of business can be likened to a game. To become a _master_ student you must not only play the game—i.e., be a student—you must also devote time and energy to learning how to play it. The first step in playing the game of becoming a master student is to get a clear picture of what is required to become one.

What is Required to Earn a Degree in Business

So what is required? Very simply, complete the curriculum! You must pass a prescribed set of courses—which, in turn, means you must pass each course in the prescribed set. And what is required to pass each course? Primarily passing a series of requirements. A requirement may be in the form of a homework assignment, an exam, an individual project, a group project, a research paper, or even an oral presentation. And to pass a series of requirements, you must pass each requirement one at a time. So by breaking it down this way, you can see that to be successful you must become a master at passing requirements such as homework, exams, papers, and projects.

Easier Said than Done

Of course, this is easier said than done, because many other factors are involved.

You must **get your life situation together**, so that you are not overburdened with problems and distractions.

You must **develop a high level of commitment and motivation** so you are willing to make the necessary choices and personal sacrifices.

You must **appreciate the value** of your business education.

You must learn how the educational system works and **how to be effective** as a student.

The purpose of this book is to give you some ideas and perspectives on these and other issues that you must address in order to be an effective student. This book focuses on the non-academic aspects of being a student. It will not increase your knowledge of mathematics or accounting or finance or management or marketing, but it can aid you in adjusting your attitude and approach so that you will be better able to learn these subjects.

Learning to be efficient and effective at the task of studying business will have enormous payoffs for you. Not only will it enhance your success as a student, it will provide you with the skills you need to be effective as a business professional. Many of the approaches you learn in this book will work for you in whatever you do.

1.4 Why Develop a Model for Viewing Your Education?

One of the most positive and unique aspects of your college experience is that you are working for yourself to prepare yourself for your future. Consider the saying:

> # No deposit. No return.

Your education represents a tremendous deposit in your future. Your return will be in direct relation to that deposit. You must realize that whenever you take the easiest instructor, avoid a tough course, or cut a class, you're hurting yourself. Whenever you make a conscious choice to avoid learning, growing, or developing, you are not getting away with something—**you are working against yourself.**

Enhancing the Quality of Your Education

If you want to get the most out of your education, you need a solid framework from which to view it. You may think of your education primarily in terms of making good grades in the courses you are required to take. If so, you need to develop a broader view of your education. A quality education involves much more.

The purpose of the next two sections is to give you four frameworks (or models) from which to view your education. These frameworks will assist you in answering such important questions as:

What is the purpose of my education?

What should I know when I graduate?

How do I know if I am getting an excellent education?

How can I enhance the quality of my education?

Will I have the knowledge and skills to get a job?

Useful for Personal Assessment

These frameworks are also useful for personal assessment or self-evaluation. My suggestion is that you measure yourself against each category presented in these models. In other words, ask yourself on a scale of 0 to 10 (10 being high): *How would I rate myself in this category?* In areas you feel you are strong, just keep doing what you have been doing. In areas you feel you need to improve, map out a plan for self-improvement. Personal assessment and personal development plans will be discussed in more detail in Chapter 3.

1.5 Four Models

In today's tight fiscal climate, universities are being held more accountable for their productivity. Institutions are being asked to establish educational objectives and student outcomes and to show that these objectives and outcomes are being met. This process is called *institutional assessment*. It is not unlike what happens to you in your classes. Your professor sets certain educational objectives or expectations for you. At the conclusion of a term, the extent to which you meet these expectations is measured and transmitted to you in the form of a final grade. This is an assessment of your performance in the class.

A key step in your understanding of the business education system is to be aware of those attributes thought to be desirable for a graduate of your business program. Different constituencies may have slightly different views as to which attributes are important. Perhaps the three most important constituencies are the AACSB (the agency that accredits business programs), the faculty in the business college, and employers of graduates of the business program. The following sections give four models for viewing your education based on the attributes identified as most important by each of these three constituencies.

AACSB Model

The following is a list of seven attributes mandated by the International Association for Management Education, the premier accrediting body for business programs in the United States [2]. The International Association for Management Education is commonly referred to as the AACSB (an abbreviation based on its name prior to 1997). The business accreditation process is discussed in more detail in Chapter 6.

The following list identifies some of those attributes AACSB will look for in a business program. However, this list is not all inclusive. The faculty of each business school, through a mission statement, will define other attributes that its particular program is striving to impart in its graduates.

1. High ethical standards

2. Understanding of the perspectives for global/international issues

3. Understand the influence of political, social, legal and regulatory, environmental and technical issues

4. Understand the impact of demographic diversity on organizations

5. A foundation knowledge of business in Accounting, Behavioral Science, Economics, Mathematics and Statistics

6. An appropriate foundation in written and oral communication

7. The ability to use library and computing facilities

One Academic Model

Your university may have a list of attributes that it strives to impart to its students. At some institutions, these attributes are clearly articulated. At others, they are less formal and can only be deduced from the culture of the institution. They also differ from one institution to another. For example, as adapted from the University of Notre Dame bulletin [3], the faculty of the business college have identified the objectives of the business administration undergraduate program to include the following:

1. Provide students with a sound liberal arts education to include appreciation for scholarship, creativity, and innovation, and ethical behavior.

2. Foster in students a recognition of the importance of administration, management, and entrepreneurship as professions and a recognition of the responsibility to manage organizational affairs and resources in a manner that will contribute both to organizational and societal goals.

3. Inspire students to be leaders in their professions and develop the capabilities for responsibility.

   a) Broad knowledge of the structure, interrelationships and problems of a global society.

   b) Competence in analysis of business problems, in communication, and in other interpersonal skills.

   c) Comprehensive understanding of administrative functions, complexity of business, and the tools of management.

   d) Skill in using knowledge to develop creative responses to opportunities and threats faced by organizations and society.

4. Facilitate the integration of the students' professional expertise with Notre Dames' sense of values.

Employment Model

   Certainly, one of the reasons you chose business as a major is the availability of jobs. In view of this, you need to consider what factors are important to employers and work to develop yourself in these areas. The following list identifies some of the areas thought to be key factors for a new graduate during the interview/evaluation process. This list of attributes was prepared by the Collegiate Employment Research Institute at Michigan State University [4] with input from business, industries and governmental agencies employing new college graduates.

1. Academic degree and grade point averages. Without other quantifiable measures to consider, employers were limited to use of grade point averages as a basic standard for success during college and potential for achievement on the job. Degrees obtained in academic fields related to the employers' openings were important.

2. Leadership qualities. Leadership roles held by college students with extra-curricular clubs and campus activities were clues to job performance potential for employers.

3. Real-world work experience. It is very important for college students to obtain pre-professional work experience to test their potential.

4. Technical skills. New graduates who have the ability to relate their educational and internship experience to the employers' world were highly desired.

5. Personal presentation. Personality, maturity, professionalism, personal impact, good-naturedness, and personal hygiene were examples of personal presentation factors cited by employers.

6. Attitude. Employers reported these factors as significant: self-confidence, poise, self-esteem, and a portion of humility.

7. Communication skills. The ability to converse during the interview. Also important for successful job performance in most organizations were the abilities to communicate effectively with others, to perform satisfactorily as a public speaker, to write well, to listen attentively, and to positively influence others towards achievement of group goals.

8. Problem analysis and analytical thinking. Employers want proven skills, so graduates will need to cite examples. Critical thinking is also measured with problem solving situations as an element of the interview.

9. Adaptability, drive, and initiative. Enthusiastic, bright, energetic, flexible, honest, and adaptable team players were words used by employers to describe the new graduates they were seeking.

10. Preparation for interviewing. The successful interviewee must be prepared. Know the organization, be on time for the interview, be familiar with the work performed, dress the part, ask for the job, and ask good, intelligent questions.

11. Career interests. Employers wanted new graduates who were goal driven and interested in the career offerings provided by the employers.

    As you approach graduation, you will undoubtedly participate in a number of interviews with prospective employers and/or graduate schools. How you fare in those interviews will depend largely on how well you prepare yourself between now and then.   The above models represent some overlap and some differentiation of desired attributes/qualities. To be strong in each area, you must make a conscious commitment to make it happen.

Subsequent chapters in this book will provide you with guidance as to what you can do over the period of your college experience to develop yourself in these areas.

- **Chapter 2** will address academic success strategies which will ensure that you have strong scholastic qualifications.

- **Chapter 3** will provide guidance in developing your personal qualifications.

- **Chapter 4** will explain the value of active involvement in student organizations and of having business-related work experience, and how to go about building a strong record of accomplishment in both areas.

Student Involvement Model

Let's assume that you want to get an excellent education—i.e., to have the knowledge, skills, and attributes that will result in your being highly sought-after by employers. How can you guarantee that you get that education? In fact, what do we mean by "excellence" or "quality" in education? We can find an answer in the outstanding paper entitled "Involvement: The Cornerstone of Excellence" by A. W. Astin, Director of UCLA's Center for the Study of Higher Education [5].

According to Astin, an "*excellent*" education is one that maximizes students' intellectual and personal development. He says the key to students' intellectual and personal development is a high level of "*student involvement*." Astin defines student involvement as:

> **"the amount of physical and psychological energy that the student devotes to the academic experience."**

Astin gives five measures of student involvement:

1. **Time and energy devoted to studying**

2. **Time spent on campus**

3. **Participation in student organizations**

4. **Interaction with faculty members**

5. **Interaction with other students**

Put simply by Astin:

> *"A highly involved student is one who, for example, devotes considerable energy to studying, spends a lot of time on campus, participates actively in student organizations, and interacts frequently with faculty members and other students."*

Conversely, according to Astin:

> *"An uninvolved student may neglect studies, spend little time on campus, abstain from extracurricular activities, and have little contact with faculty members or other students."*

Which of these statements best describes you? Evaluate yourself against Astin's five measures. In this way, you can assess the quality of your education and identify areas where you can improve.

The Astin *student involvement* model indicates that the approach you take will play a critical role in ensuring that you get a quality education. Although your institution can do things to encourage you to study more, to spend more time on campus, to become involved in student organizations, to interact with your professors, and to interact with fellow students, to a great extent increasing your level of involvement up to you.

You can choose to devote more time and energy to your studies, to spend more time on campus, and to become active in student organizations. And you can choose to interact more with your professors and to become more involved with other students. In doing so, you will greatly enhance the quality of your education.

1.6 *Preview of Later Chapters*

In later chapters, we'll address these topics in more detail. The following questions will be answered.

⇒Just how much study time is required and how do you organize that study time for maximum effectiveness?

⇒What are the advantages of spending more time on campus and immersing yourself in the academic environment of the institution?

⇒What resources does being on campus allow you to access and how do you go about making optimal use of those resources?

⇒What are the educational benefits of participation in extracurricular activities and student organizations?

⇒How can you develop your organizational and leadership skills through that participation?

We will place particular emphasis on what increasing your interaction with faculty can do to enhance the quality of your education. Specifically, we will address these questions:

⇒What can faculty offer to you in addition to classroom instruction?

⇒What approaches will be effective in developing helpful relationships with faculty?

Finally, we will put forth the perspective that of all the resources available to you, the most valuable one is your peers. To assist you in making effective use of your peers, we will address the following questions:

⇒ What benefits will come to you from building academic relationships with other students?

⇒ How can you best utilize your peers for the purposes of sharing information and engaging in collaborative learning and group study?

Summary

The purpose of this chapter was to introduce you to the keys to success in studying business. Three primary traits that lead to success were discussed:

1. Your determination to persist even in the face of adversity.

2. The amount of effort you put in, in terms of both time on task and energy and mental power.

3. The approach that you take.

The next chapter will put forth strategies and approaches that will enhance your effectiveness as a student. Success requires not only that you "study harder" but also that you "study smarter."

Four models (or frameworks) were presented that can assist you in understanding what knowledge and skills you're seeking to develop through your business education, as well as behaviors that will give you that "excellent" education.

1. The AACSB Attributes Model

2. One Academic Model

3. The Employment Model

4. The Student Involvement Model

Each of these models provides specific categories against which you can measure yourself. No one model is being promoted as the "best," but rather the combination of all models will help to achieve an overall excellent education. This type of personal assessment will help you identify your strengths and weaknesses. Strengths can be used to your advantage, and once weaknesses are identified, self-improvement plans can be developed and implemented.

References

1. Jacobs, Joseph J., *The Anatomy of an Entrepreneur*, ICS Press, Institute for Contemporary Studies, San Francisco, CA, 1991.

2. Achieving Quality and Improvement through Self-Evaluation and Peer Review, Standards for Accreditation Business and Accounting Handbook, Revised April 12, 1994. (Available from AACSB, 600 Emerson Road, Suite 300, St Louis, MO 63141-6762).

3. University of Notre Dame Undergraduate Programs, "1997-98 Bulletin of Information," 1 Grace Hall, University of Notre Dame, Notre Dame, IN 46556 .

4. Scheetz, L. Patrick, "Recruiting Trends 1997-98," Collegiate Employment Research Institute, Michigan State University, 113 Student Services Building, East Lansing, MI 48824-1113.

5. Astin, Alexander W., "Involvement" The Cornerstone of Excellence," *Change*, July/August 1985.

Exercises

1. How many hours do you think you should study for each hour of class time in your business courses? Is this the same for all courses? If not, list four factors that determine how much you need to study in a specific class.

2. List ten goals you want to achieve in your lifetime. Classify each as a short-term goal, intermediate-term goal, or long-term goal.

3. Do you have a personal goal of graduating with your bachelor's degree in business? How important is that goal to you? How can you make it more important?

4. List ten benefits that will come to you when you are successful in graduating in business. Rank them in order of importance.

5. Have any of your teachers or professors ever done anything to make you feel as though you couldn't make it? What did they do? Why do you think they did that?

6. Have you ever achieved anything through sheer determination that others thought you couldn't? What was it?

7. Do you believe the statement, "You learn more from your failures than from your successes"? Can you give an example from your own life? What did you learn from that experience?

8. Do you think that people succeed because of their ability or because of their effort? Which do you think is more important: ability or effort? Why?

9. List five things that you could do to study "smarter" that you are not currently doing. Pick the two most important ones and try to implement them.

10. Would you rather tackle an easy problem or a difficult one? Which do you think benefits you the most? Make an analogy with the task of developing your physical strength.

11. List ten tasks that a business professional might perform (e.g., write a report, conduct a meeting). Rank them in the order that you would most enjoy doing them. Now rank them in the importance your employer would assign. Compare the lists and explain the similarity/differences between the top three.

12. First rate <u>yourself</u> on a scale of 0 to 10 (10 being high) on the following and then rate the items on the level of importance on a scale of 0 to 10 (10 being high):

Item	Description	Rating	Importance
a.	Writing skills		
b.	Oral communications skills		
c.	Ability to work with other people		
d.	Commitment to becoming a professional business person		
e.	Professional and ethical standards		
f.	Positive attitude toward life		
g.	Computer skills		
h.	Proficiency in mathematics		
I.	Participation in student organizations		
j.	Degree you work collaboratively with other students		
k.	Time and energy devoted to studying		
l.	Time spent on campus		
m.	Overall grade point average		

13. Which of the items in #12 have to do with your skills? With your attitude? With your approach to your studies?

14. Pick the three things from #12 that need your greatest attention and three things that need your least attention. Develop a plan for self-improvement for those that need your greatest attention. Implement the plan.

These need my greatest attention	These need my least attention
1.	1.
2.	2.
3.	3.

15. List ten skills or attributes that you need to work effectively with other people. How can you go about acquiring these skills and attributes?

16. List six things that your professors can do for you in addition to providing you with classroom instruction.

17. Find out whether your business college has a list of attributes it strives to impart to its graduates. This may be part of the college's mission statement. How does it compare with the information in Section 1.5?

18. Ask one of your professors why he or she chose teaching as a career rather than working in business or industry.

19. If you spend 100 hours studying, how many of those hours would you be studying alone? How many would you be studying with at least one other student? If you study primarily alone, why? List three benefits of working collaboratively with other students.

20. Determine where in your business curriculum you will develop the following skills:

Skill	Place in Curriculum
Teamwork	
Database Management/Analysis	
Judgement/Decision Making	
Ethical/Social Responsibility	
Communication Skills (writing, speaking, and listening)	
Business Applications Software	

Chapter 2
ACADEMIC SUCCESS STRATEGIES

Introduction

The purpose of this chapter is to present those strategies and approaches that are most important to your academic success. Much of the material in this chapter was originally published in Reference 1, and it has been adapted for business students.

We will first discuss the importance of establishing short-term, intermediate-term, and long-term goals. We will then discuss the need for you to structure various aspects of your life so that you can accomplish your primary goal of graduating in business. By establishing a realistic workload for yourself, you will be able to take advantage of key resources available to enhance the quality of your education.

Next we will address perhaps the most important of these resources—your peers. Making effective use of your peers through collaborative learning and group study will be a critical factor in your success as a student and in the quality of the education you receive.

We will then present strategies for making effective use of your professors both in and out of the classroom. Ways of making effective use of your peers and your professors expands on Astin's Student Involvement Model presented in Chapter 1.

Finally, we will consider those study skills that are particularly important in math and business courses. These include your overall approach to subject mastery, time management, and strategies for preparing for and taking tests.

2.1 Set Goals for Yourself

Obvious though it may sound, setting goals—having a clear idea of what you want to accomplish in both the short and long term—is a key requirement to becoming an effective student and a successful professional. Only when you set goals will you have something to strive for and something against which to measure yourself.

Goals Give You Something to Measure Yourself Against

Consider, for example, two business students in a calculus class who score a *B* on their first exam. One student is extremely unhappy and resolves to study much harder for the next test. She has set a goal of earning an *A* in the course and by falling short on the first test, she knows that she must study harder. The other student, however, is more than satisfied with the *B* grade and decides that he may be able to increase his work hours since even less study is necessary than he has been doing. These different behaviors are the result of different expectations—of the two students having different goals for themselves. As this case of the two students illustrates, success or failure can only be measured according to self-imposed goals.

Astronaut Franklin Chang-Diaz

Franklin Chang-Diaz was born and grew up in Costa Rica. As a child, he was enamored of the U.S. space program. He and his friends built spacecraft out of cardboard boxes, equipping them with broken radios and furniture. They would go through a countdown and lift-off and pretend they traveled to a distant planet. Because of his interest, he set a personal goal of becoming a U.S. astronaut! Imagine a young Costa Rican citizen who didn't speak a word of English aspiring to be a U.S. astronaut.

When Chang-Diaz finished high school, he worked for a year and saved enough money to buy a one-way airplane ticket to Hartford, Connecticut where he had some distant relatives. In Hartford he repeated his senior year of high school, learned English, and was admitted to the University of Connecticut. After graduating with honors, he began graduate study at MIT, eventually receiving his Ph.D. in plasma physics. He then applied for the astronaut program, was accepted, and became the U.S.'s first Hispanic astronaut. He flew his first space shuttle mission in January 1986.

The point that the story of Dr. Chang-Diaz drives home so convincingly is the need to have goals. For how can you expect to get someplace if you don't know where it is you want to go? This is something you must define for yourself, just as Dr. Chang-Diaz did for himself.

Write Down Your Goals

Right now your most important goal is to graduate with your degree in business. But what else would you like to accomplish? Become president of your own company? Make a million dollars? Become a college professor? And what about your more immediate goals? Maybe you want to make a 3.0 GPA next semester, improve your writing skills, or become president of a campus student organization.

I would suggest that you go through an exercise of writing down short-term, intermediate-term, and long-term goals. Consider what you want to accomplish in the next week, in the next month, in the next year, in the next five years. Review these lists regularly and revise them as necessary. Measure yourself against your goals and adjust your behavior to bring your actions in line with them.

Make achieving your goals important to you. Above all, make the goal of graduating with a degree in business your number one priority. Few other accomplishments will have such a profound positive effect on your life.

2.2 Structure Your Life Situation: Don't Program Yourself for Failure

Setting a goal is easy. Most people would like to be rich, to be successful, to have good personal relationships with others. You may want to do something significant for the benefit of mankind. The difficult part is to act in such a way as to ensure that a particular goal is reached. People who want to have a lot of money, for example, must behave in such a way as to bring this about. They must concentrate on such matters as preparing themselves to be able to earn money and learning how to invest wisely. They may need to defer their immediate desires—such as buying a car, taking a vacation, or buying a large screen entertainment center—in pursuit of their longer term, more important goal of acquiring and building wealth.

Make Your Goal of Graduating Important

In like manner, setting a goal of graduating in business is easy. Making it happen is the hard part. One of the most difficult but important aspects of being a successful student is to structure your life situation so that school can become your number one priority. To be a full-time student is a major commitment. If you devote the appropriate amount of time and effort to your studies, you will have limited time or energy for other obligations.

There are a number of factors outside of school—family, friends, and work, commuting—that can place major demands on you. It is imperative that you do whatever is necessary to minimize the impact of these factors. I have seen students who take a full load of courses, commute over an hour each way to school, work 20 hours a week, have a family that expects them to help out around the house, and try to maintain an active social life. Most students in this situation are programmed for failure.

Living Arrangements

If at all possible, live on or near the university campus. The more immersed you can get in the university environment, the better your chances of success. Commuting takes time, energy, and money; and living at home can present distractions. Parents may expect you to help around the house. Little brothers and sisters may be noisy and distracting. Neighborhood friends may not understand your need to study. Above all, whether you live at home or on campus, this is a time in your life when it's appropriate to be a bit selfish. Place a high value on your time, and learn to say no when necessary.

Part-time Work

Full-time business study is a full-time commitment. Working up to twelve hours a week is probably okay, but more is almost certain to take its toll on your academic performance. While it may be essential for you to work, it may also be that you are working to afford a nice car, stereo, or other non-essentials. Look at it this way. You may get a job for $6 an hour now, but in doing so you jeopardize your education or at best extend the time to graduation. The average starting salary for business graduates is around $16 an hour. So try to delay as many material wants as possible. You will have much more in the long term.

If you must work more than 12 hours a week, I would recommend that you reduce your course load. The following is given as a guide.

Hours worked	Max. course load
12 hrs/wk	full load
20 hrs/wk	12 units
40 hrs/wk	8 units

I often meet students who are taking six courses each term and only completing four or five of them. When I suggest that they reduce their course load, they respond "I can't do that. I'd never get finished with my degree!" Obviously, they are only moving through the curriculum at the rate of courses completed, not courses attempted. And their GPA is declining! The point is be realistic about your situation. Don't create an unmanageable workload and then kid yourself into thinking that it is working.

Influence of Friends, Family

Friends and family may not understand the demands of a college curriculum and may unintentionally distract you. Have a frank talk with your parents. Let them know that you want to make school your number one priority. Ask for their help, and negotiate clear agreements about their demands on you.

If you are a recent high school graduate, dealing with friends from high school—especially those who are not pursuing an education—may be a problem for you. They may put pressure on you to spend as much time with them as you did in high school, while you may find that you have less and less in common with them. Ideally, you should concentrate on developing new relationships with students who are engaged in the same coursework as you. This will benefit you since these friends will support you in your academic endeavors and you will no longer have to separate your academic life from your social life. This does not mean you must abandon your old friends but rather expand your circle of friends to include your new academic life. Visit with your non-college friends during breaks and summers.

2.3 Benefits of Collaborative Learning and Group Study

As a student, you are an active participant in the *teaching/learning process*. The university focuses primarily on the *teaching* part of this process. For the most part, the *learning* part is left up to you.

Teaching Structures

A number of well-known structures are in place to accomplish teaching. These include: large sections where one professor lectures to 300 or 500 students; small sections where one professor lectures 25 to 30 students; recitations or tutorials where a teaching assistant works problems for 10 to 15 students; and one-on-one tutoring where a tutor works with a single student.

These teaching structures have several common features. First, all involve a person who is knowledgeable in a subject (an "expert" if you will) communicating what he or she knows to a less knowledgeable person (you, the student). Unfortunately, most of the communication is one-way, i.e., from the teacher to the student. And more importantly, very little learning takes place in these teaching structures. The limitations of the "lecture" format of instruction can be underscored by the following interpretation of what goes on there:

> *The information passes from the notes of the professor to the notes of the student without passing through the mind of either one.*

Learning Structures

And then we have *learning structures*. There are only two:

1) Solitary

2) Collaborative

Either you do it alone, or you do it with others. Whenever I talk with a student, I always ask, "What fraction of your study time is spent on a regular basis studying with at least one other student?" Generally less than 10 percent of the students I see study on a regular basis with another student or group of students.

My anecdotal study indicates that if left to their own discretion about 90 percent of business students do virtually 100 percent of their studying alone. Hence, the primary learning structure involves a student sitting alone mastering knowledge and applying that knowledge to the completion of assignments.

There are reasons why students study alone. I often ask students who indicate that they study primarily alone: "Why don't you work with other students on your academic work?" Three answers are most commonly given:

1. *I learn more studying by myself.*

2. *It is too hard to coordinate study time with someone else.*

3. *It's not right. You're supposed to do your own work.*

The fact that most students study alone is indeed unfortunate because research shows that students who engage in collaborative learning and group study perform better academically, persist longer, improve their communication skills, feel better about their educational experience, and have enhanced self-esteem. According to Professor Karl A. Smith at the University of Minnesota, a nationally recognized expert on cooperative learning [3]:

Cooperation among students typically results in:

(a) higher achievement and greater productivity,
(b) more caring, supportive, and committed relationships,
(c) greater psychological health, social competence,
   and self-esteem.

There are three very powerful and persuasive reasons why you should engage in collaborative learning and group study:

You'll be better prepared for the business "work world."

You'll learn more.

You'll enjoy it more.

You'll Be Better Prepared for the Business "Work World"

Whether you choose to study alone or with others most likely depends on what you think is the purpose of an education. If you think the purpose of an education is to develop your proficiency at sitting alone mastering knowledge and applying that knowledge to the solution of problems, then you have defined it that way and that's what you should do. However, I can assure you that it is unlikely that anyone will pay you money to do that. That's not what business professionals do by and large.

So if you spend your four or five years of business study primarily sitting alone mastering knowledge and applying that knowledge to the solution of problems (and perhaps even becoming very good at it!), you will have missed out on much of what a quality education should be. A quality education should provide you not only the ability to learn and to apply what you learn, but also with the ability to communicate what you have learned to others. You should acquire the ability to explain your ideas to others and to listen to others explain their ideas to you and to understand them. You should have the ability to engage and contribute to dialogues and discussions on problem formulation and problem solutions. You may have the greatest idea going, but if you can't convince others of it, it is unlikely that your idea will be implemented.

You'll Learn More

The second reason I would strongly encourage you to engage regularly in collaborative learning and group study is that you will learn more. There are a number of ways to look at this idea. One is the adage: *"Two minds are better than one."* Through collaborative study not only will more information be brought to bear, but also you will have the opportunity to see others' thought processes at work. Perhaps you have played the game *Trivial Pursuit*. It always amazes me how a small group of people working together can come up with the answer to a question that no one member of the group working alone could have.

Another idea comes from the statement "If you ever want to really learn a subject, teach it." As an undergraduate business student, I took various courses in management theory. I did not really understand the subject until I first taught it. When two students work together collaboratively, in effect, half the time one student is teaching the other and the other half of the time the roles are reversed.

You'll Enjoy it More

Finally, group study is more fun, and because you'll enjoy it more, you are likely to do more of it. I often conduct small in-class projects that involve collaborative learning. At some point during the process I will have one half of the class work on a problem in small groups and the other half work alone on the very same problem. After about ten minutes, the individuals who are working alone are looking at their watches and seem restless and bored. When time is called after twenty minutes, those who are working in groups are disappointed and ask for more time. They often express that they are just getting "hot" on the problem. The next day when I ask "How many of you continued thinking about, working on, or talking to others about the problem we did yesterday?" most of those who worked in groups raise their hands, whereas those who worked alone do not.

REAL LIFE ADVENTURES by Gary Wise and Lance Aldrich

HEY, I'VE GOT AN IDEA! INSTEAD OF GOING TO THE PARTY, LET'S STUDY!

Campus radical.

REAL LIFE ADVENTURES © GarLanco
Reprinted with permission of UNIVERSAL
PRESS SYNDICATE

The cartoon on the previous page illustrates the true value of academic relationships.

Frequently Asked Questions about Collaborative Learning

Several questions are frequently asked about collaborative learning:

- **What percentage of your study time should be done in groups?**
- **What is the ideal size of a study group?**
- **What can be done to keep the group from getting off task?**

There are no definitive answers to these questions. And, the answers will vary from individual to individual.

Certainly, you should not spend all of your study time working collaboratively. I would suggest somewhere between 25 percent and 50 percent. Prior to coming together, each member of a group should review the material and work some problems to gain a base level of proficiency. The purpose of the group work should be to refine and deepen that base level of understanding. The better prepared the group members are prior to coming together, the more can be accomplished through the group interaction.

When you hear the term "group study," what size group do you think of? Five? Ten? Fifteen? My ideal study group is **two or three**. When two or three people work together, it is possible for each to be the "teacher" for a significant amount of time. In larger groups, I always feel like I must compete to get some of the time. Even among study partners, a conscious effort may be required to keep one of the partners from dominating the dialogue. If more people come together to study, it's okay. Generally subgroups of twos or threes will develop anyway.

You may find it difficult to stay on task when working with others. I have no answer to the issue of how to stay on task except to just do it. Personally, I find it much easier to stay on task when working with a study partner than when working alone. One approach is to predefine the study goal for the day—it may be a chapter, a set of problems, or a complex topic. Whatever your study goal is, it will help you to concentrate your efforts, give you a sense of purpose, and most of all provide you with a measurable accomplishment. I would also recommend structured breaks. Agree, for example, to study for one hour and then take a fifteen-minute break. Then back to work. When all is said and done, staying on task is a matter of discipline and your commitment to your education.

New Paradigm

The idea of collaborative learning is consistent with modern business management practices and with what representatives of business and industry tell us they want in our graduates. *Collaboration* and *cooperation* represent a shift in the *competitive* paradigm of the past. W. Edwards Deming, father of the "quality" movement, makes a compelling case: [3]

> *We have grown up in a climate of competition between people, teams, departments, divisions, pupils, schools, and universities. Economists have taught us that competition will solve our problems. Actually, competition, we see now, is destructive. It would be better if everyone would work together as a system, with the aim for everybody to win. What we need is cooperation and transformation to a new style of management . . . Competition leads to loss. People pulling in opposite directions on a rope only exhaust themselves. They go nowhere. What we need is cooperation.*
>
> *Every example of cooperation is one of benefit and gains to them that cooperate. Cooperation is especially productive in a system well managed.*

2.4 Making Effective Use of Your Professors

Your professors represent an extremely valuable resource to you. They can provide you with individual help in your courses, give you advice about the curriculum, and advise you concerning regulations and procedures. Professors can also counsel you about business careers, write letters of recommendation for you, and be supportive in numerous other ways.

The first step in making effective use of your professors is to overcome any fear or intimidation of them you may feel. Being awed by your professors is a natural first reaction since they are older and better educated, and often project a confident, "know it all" attitude. As a result, you may think that your professors don't care about you or even that they are against you. But this is probably not true. After all, most professors chose an academic career because they like teaching and enjoy working with students. And remember that professors are human beings just like you. They have similar needs, fears, and insecurities as you. They may very much need to be liked, want you to think they are good teachers, or even feel the need to impress you with their knowledge.

The need to make effective use of both your peers and your professors is supported by a quote from the preface of an excellent study of the teaching/learning process conducted at Harvard University [4]:

> *Is there any common theme that faculty members can use to help students, and indeed that students can use to help themselves? The answer is a strong yes. All the specific findings point to, and illustrate, one main idea. It is that students who get the most out of college, who grow the most academically, and who are the happiest, organize their time to include interpersonal activities with faculty members, or with fellow students, built around substantive academic work.*

Your professors may be primarily focused on the formal teaching process. Most are committed to a lecture style of teaching in which they convey knowledge to you in a one-way communication style. Most likely, they assign homework problems for you to do. Ideally, they collect and grade the problems, providing you with valuable feedback. Professors also establish the basis for your final grade in the course—generally your scores on one or more tests, your score on a project, and a final examination. This process of professor lecturing, students doing homework and exams to evaluate level of mastery of subject matter, is the general conception of the *teaching/learning process.*

Important Roles for Your Professors

But your professors can contribute much more than this to your overall education process. They can provide you with invaluable one-on-one instruction. They can give you academic advising, career guidance, and personal advice. Professors can monitor your progress and hold you accountable for your performance. They can help you find a summer job in industry and even hire you on their research grants. They can serve as a valuable reference in your process of applying for employment either while you are a student or when you graduate. They can nominate you for scholarships or academic awards.

Value of One-on-One Instruction

Of these, perhaps most valuable is one-on-one instruction. Without question, the best way to learn is to engage in a one-on-one dialogue with an expert in a subject. This is one of the oldest and most effective forms of teaching and is known as the *Socratic method* because it was the primary form of teaching used by the Greek philosopher Socrates. Our present system where one teacher lectures to 30 (or sometimes 300!) students is obviously not most effective for the learning process, but we do it that way to be cost-effective.

Having one teacher for each student would be ideal, but it would be too expensive. The primary advantage of the *Socratic method* is that, through the dialogue between the teacher and student, the teacher can know at once whether the student understands and can adjust his or her approach accordingly. I would encourage you to seek every possible opportunity for this kind of teaching.

Take Responsibility for Winning Over Your Professors

How can you be successful in getting those things from your professors beyond classroom instruction that will enhance your education? Often students complain that their professors don't have time for them and don't seem to want to help them. What is your role in this interaction? In my experience, many students approach professors from the "Me, Me, Me; I want, I want, I want; Give me, Give me, Give me" perspective. It is no wonder that professors give so little when approached in this way. Would you?

The real question is how can you go about winning over your professors so that they want to help you. Perhaps the "bible" in winning people over is the classic book by Dale Carnegie: *How to Win Friends and Influence People* [5]. Written in 1936, this book has stood the test of time and is still a best seller. I would commend it to you as an excellent resource for you to improve your "people" skills. Dale Carnegie's "Six Ways to Make People Like You" provides a good starting point for winning over your professors:

Six Ways to Make People Like You

Rule 1	Become genuinely interested in other people.
Rule 2	Smile.
Rule 3	Remember that a person's name is to him or her the sweetest and most important sound in any language.
Rule 4	Be a good listener. Encourage others to talk about themselves.
Rule 5	Talk in terms of the other person's interest.
Rule 6	Make the other person feel important—and do it sincerely.

Dale Carnegie's book is filled with anecdotes. Most are "dated" and that aspect underscores the timeliness of their message. The one I like the best is as follows:

C. M. Knaphle, Jr., of Philadelphia, had tried for years to sell coal to a large chain-store organization. But the chain-store company continued to purchase its fuel from an out-of-town dealer and continued to haul it right past the door of Knaphle's office. Mr. Knaphle made a speech one night before one of my classes, pouring out his hot wrath upon chain stores, branding them a curse to the nation. And still he wondered why he couldn't sell them.

I suggested that he try different tactics. To put it briefly this is what happened. We staged a debate between members of the course on "Resolve that the spread of the chain store is doing the country more harm than good."

Knaphle, at my suggestion, took the negative side; he agreed to defend the chain stores, and then went straight to an executive of the chain-store organization that he despised and said: "I am not here to try to sell coal. I have come to you for help because I can't think of anyone else who would be more capable of giving me the facts I want. I am anxious to win this debate; and I'll deeply appreciate whatever help you can give me."

Here is the rest of the story in Mr. Knaphle's own words:

I had asked this man for precisely one minute of his time. It was with that understanding that he consented to see me. After I had stated my case, he motioned me to a chair and talked to me for exactly one hour and forty-seven minutes. He called in another executive who had written a book on chain stores. He wrote to the National Chain Store Association and secured for me a copy of a debate on the subject. He feels that the chain store is rendering a real service to humanity. He is proud of what he is doing for hundreds of communities. His eyes fairly glowed as he talked; and I must confess that he opened my eyes to things to things I had never even dreamed of. He changed my whole mental attitude. As I was leaving, he walked with me to the door, put his arm around my shoulder, wished me well in my debate, and asked me to stop in and see him again and let him know how I made out. The last words he said to me were: "Please see me again later in the spring. I should like to place an order with you for coal."

To me that was almost a miracle. Here he was offering to buy coal without my even suggesting it. I had made more headway in two hours by becoming genuinely interested in him and his problems than I could have made in ten years by trying to get him interested in my coal and me.

I hope by now you have seen the moral of this anecdote, and more importantly, it has given you ideas as to how to approach your professors. This anecdote and Dale Carnegie's "Six Ways to Make People Like You" both emphasize the importance of showing interest in others and of approaching them from their perspective.

Just as Dale Carnegie knew Mr. Knaphle could win over the chain store executive by appealing to his need to promote the interest of chain stores, there are three characteristics of professors that you can use to win them over:

---

1. They believe their areas of specialty are critically important and extremely interesting.

2. They have chosen to devote their career to academia rather than professional practice and they believe they are outstanding teachers.

3. They don't call them "professors" for nothing. They have lots of knowledge and love to convey it to others.

Your challenge as a student is to avoid doing things that conflict with these characteristics of professors, and rather, to do things which support them.

Behaviors to Avoid

What behaviors conflict with the professor's attitude that his or her specialty is interesting and important? We could make a long list.

Coming late to class
Sleeping in class
Talking in class
Doing other homework in class
Leaving class early
Failing to do the assigned homework
Asking how many class meetings you are allowed to miss

I'm sure you can add to this list. These and other behaviors also send professors signals that you don't feel they are good teachers. Examples of these other behaviors are correcting professors' mistakes in an antagonistic tone, complaining that exams are too hard or that grading is unfair, or sending non-verbal messages to your professors that you do not like them. One sure way to antagonize is to make every visit to your professor's office a complaint session or a time to ask for special favors.

Winning Behaviors

You can win over your professors by sending them messages that you feel that the subject is interesting and important and that you value them as a teacher. Practicing the opposite of the behaviors listed in the previous paragraph would be a good start.

Be on time to class
Sit in the front
Pay attention
Ask questions
Apply yourself to the assigned homework
Attend all scheduled class periods

But there is a much more direct way. Just tell them! In my experience, professors get far too few compliments. I'm not sure why students are so reluctant to tell professors that they like the course, are interested in the subject, or appreciate the good job they are doing in teaching the class. I can assure you that doing so will go a long way toward winning over your professors.

Another way to develop a positive relationship with your professors is to show that you are interested in them. Try this approach. Go see one of your professors during her office hours and ask a question about her. "Where did you go to college?" "How did you decide to become a professor?" "How did you choose your discipline?" Generally, students report very positive experiences from such interactions.

2.5 Utilizing Tutors and Other Campus Resources

Your university provides a number of student services to support your education. These include tutoring, career planning and placement, personal counseling, learning assistance, financial aid, and health services. These services are generally free to you. In fact, you are paying for them through your tuition and fees. However, receiving the benefits of these campus services requires that you take the initiative. They will not seek you out. Part of good *academic gamesmanship,* then, is for you to scope out the resources available to you and make optimal use of them.

Tutoring

Tutors are another excellent source of the one-on-one instruction discussed in a previous section. Some students have a resistance to utilizing tutors; viewing the need for tutoring as an admission they are doing poorly or need help. I would encourage you to take a positive attitude toward the use of tutors. Look upon tutoring as an opportunity for you to have a dialogue with an expert in a subject that you want to learn.

Your university may provide tutoring services through a variety of sources. Tutoring may be available through a learning assistance center. Your mathematics department may run a math lab, or members of your business honor society Beta Gamma Sigma may do voluntary tutoring as a service to the college. If free tutoring is not available, you might find listings for tutors available for hire from your advisor, your department chair, or the placement office. You may want to ask an upperclass student to help you. Lots of students take pride in sharing their knowledge.

Other Important Campus Resources

Many other campus services are available to you. The **career planning and placement office** can provide you with information about businesses, help you prepare a resume, work with you to develop your interviewing skills, and help you find summer jobs. The **counseling center** can assist you with personal problems, both those related to your academics—such as lack of motivation, inability to concentrate, and test anxiety—and those that are non-academic, such as family, financial, and legal problems. The **learning assistance center** can help you improve your reading, writing, and study skills. Your **financial aid office** can inform you about scholarships and loans for which you might be eligible. Your **student health center** can help you with physical or emotional problems. Remember, though, most of these campus services require that you take the initiative. You will need to seek them out.

2.6 Develop Your Study Skills

How you do in school is a direct result of the approach you take to the process of studying and learning. Becoming a *master student* means that you have mastered the principles of good study skills and are able to put them into daily practice.

The area of study skills is extremely broad and many full-length books on it have been written. Topics covered include note taking, test taking, reading for comprehension, time management, and many others. It is not my intention here to give any sort of complete coverage on this subject, but rather to emphasize a few critical ideas which, if put into practice, would dramatically enhance your academic success.

"Take It as It Comes"

I use this well-known expression to emphasize what I consider to be the **key** to success in business study. Put more directly:

> **Don't allow the next class session in a course to come
> without having mastered the material presented in the
> previous session.**

Have you ever thought of why a typical course meets for one hour three times a week for 15 weeks? The answer is obvious. We can only absorb a certain amount of material at one time, and only when that material is mastered can we go on to new material. The faculty have designed a sound educational experience in which they sequentially cover small amounts of material for you to master. However, unless you do your part, you can transform the sound educational experience into an unsound one.

A common mistake is to study from test to test rather than from class to class. One trap you can fall into is to be lulled into a false sense of security because the teacher presents the material so clearly that you feel you understand it completely and therefore do not need to study it. But when you attend a lecture that is presented quite clearly, it only proves that the **teacher** understands the material. What is necessary is for **you** to understand it—for **you** to be able to give the lecture. In fact, that should be your goal in every class. Get to the point where you could give the lecture.

To do this requires that you read your text, study your notes, solve as many problems as time permits, and discuss the subject with others. But the key is timing. For effective and efficient learning, it is essential that this occur before the next class meeting in the course. Research on learning indicates that more efficient learning occurs the sooner studying takes place after the initial exposure to the material. Certainly, then, you should not wait for three weeks until a test is announced to begin studying the material. It is better to study the same evening rather than the next day.

Learning is a Reinforcement Process

Real learning and understanding only come after repeated exposure to the subject matter. The way in which we learn the subject of mathematics can serve as an example.

Our first exposure to mathematics was in grade school. We continued our studies in junior high. In high school the requirements continued with algebra, geometry, and trigonometry and in some cases pre-calculus. In college, we study statistics and calculus and their application to business problems. Mathematics is integrated into a majority of our courses in college and for a thorough understanding of business and the value of mathematics we could pursue graduate study—a master's or even Ph.D. degree. Even then, if we were to begin teaching business we would find areas where we were not completely clear and probably only after a number of years of teaching would we feel that we had total mastery of just the basics of the subject.

Even for the brightest person, learning is a slow process that occurs over time and relies on repeated reinforcements. Given the example of how we learn the subject of *mathematics,* it is surprising that students feel they can "cram" in the material the night before the test.

The educational system is structured to offer you the opportunity to reinforce the subject matter many times within the semester or quarter. Only by taking advantage of these opportunities will you achieve a satisfactory level of learning.

Your first exposure to the material would ideally come when you read over the material ***prior*** to the lecture. Preparing for lectures is an outstanding strategy if you want to be a master student. You will get a lot more out of the lectures, and the lecture then becomes a first reinforcement rather than your first exposure to the material.

To get the most out of the lecture, sit near the front, concentrate on the material being presented, and take thorough notes. Good note taking is an art, as you have to balance the processes of taking notes and listening at the same time. Writing down the material will further reinforce learning, and good notes will provide you a record of what the professor feels is important. Also, when you are preparing for a test having good notes will prevent you from spending time studying material that is in the text but was not covered in class.

As previously discussed, study the material as soon as possible after the lecture. Review and annotate your notes; read any text material related to the lecture; and work end of chapter exercises or problems—as many as you can ***not just the assigned problems***. Solving one or two problems, even though that may be all the professor assigned, will not ensure an adequate level of understanding. If time permits work <u>all</u> of the problems in the book. If more time is available, work them a second time. Practice, practice, practice! The more problems you solve, the more you will learn.

> **Most of the learning in business courses comes not from studying or reading but from solving problems.**

Once you have done these things, you will be ready for the next class meeting. You will have already had a number of reinforcements of the material. Later you will again reinforce the material when you review for a test and still later when you prepare for the final exam.

How Many Hours Should You Study?

Once you commit to keeping up in your classes and taking advantage of each opportunity to reinforce the learning process, you must determine how many hours of study to put in to master the material covered in a one-hour lecture. I'm sure you've heard the standard rule-of-thumb that you should study three hours out of class for every hour in class. No way! This is a gross oversimplification. The truth is that you should put in whatever amount of time you need. For demanding courses it is doubtful that three hours are enough. The correct number for you may be three, four, or even five hours.

Even though it is difficult to assess initially, I suggest that you come up with a number for each of your classes. In making this determination, you will have to consider such factors as:

How difficult is this course?

How good a student you are?

How well prepared you are for the course?

What grade you want to receive?

Making an *A* will take a lot more effort than making a *C*.

Once you have decided that for a particular course you should study say three hours between one class meeting and the next and you realize that the best time to do this studying is as soon after you have attended the lecture as possible, you have done the easy part. The hard part is actually doing it. Putting these approaches into practice requires you to be an organized person and an expert at managing your time.

Learn to Manage Your Time.

Everyone from Bill Gates, the president of Microsoft Corporation, to a homeless person has exactly the same amount of time—to be precise, 168 hours per week. There is no point in saying that you have no time because you have just as much as anyone else does. Some people, however, accomplish a great deal with their time and others accomplish virtually nothing. Those who accomplish a great deal, without exception, value their time and have a system for scheduling and managing their time. Some of these systems are very sophisticated and you may wish to look into acquiring one of them, particularly once you become a business professional. As a student, you can do quite well with a daily calendar to record your appointments and with a simple form (like the one at the end of this chapter) for scheduling your time.

Your effectiveness as a student will be greatly enhanced by scheduling your time. The approach I took when I was a student was two-phased—a semester schedule and a weekly update.

Phase 1. At the beginning of each semester, I would collect all my course syllabi and identify my desired major social activities (such as football games, trips home, music shows, etc.) and whatever else I anticipated for the term. I would then take this array of activities and create a semester matrix to help me identify potential time conflicts. I would add in every detail I could regarding my classes including exam dates, homework assignments, quizzes, and project due dates. Invariably, the matrix looked like a cyclic wave with peaks and valleys of activities.

I would then make as many "adjustments" as I could to eliminate or at least minimize conflicts between activities. For example if my matrix indicated I would have three exams on the Monday following a home football weekend, I would schedule my review sessions for those exams on separate days at a time prior to the football weekend. If two research papers were due on the same day, I would schedule one to be completed early and turn it in <u>early</u> (no professor ever complained about my turning in a paper early!). This process allowed me to graphically evaluate my semester workload and realistically access whether I could handle it.

Phase 2. I would sit down each Sunday night to review my semester schedule and then schedule my entire week using a form like the one shown at the end of this chapter.

I would encourage you to use this form. First, write down all your commitments: classes, meetings, outside work, time to get to and from school, time for meals, sleep and so forth. The rest of the time is available for one of two purposes—study or recreation.

Next, schedule blocks of time to study. You have already decided how much time you need between one class meeting and the next and you know the advantages of scheduling this time as soon after the class meeting as possible. Write down both <u>where</u> and <u>what</u> you will study. Students tend to waste too much time between classes making three decisions:

Should I study now or later?

Where should I study?

What should I study?

By making these decisions in advance, you will improve your efficiency tremendously.

Once your study time is scheduled, check to see if you've left open some time for recreation. You will need some time for physical activity.

> ## A healthy body leads to a healthy mind.

If you do not have time for recreation, you probably are over-committed. You have taken on too much. Remember one of the advantages of making a schedule is that it gives you a graphic picture of your situation. Don't "program yourself for failure." Be realistic about what you can handle. If you are over-committed, you may want to choose to let something go. Reduce your work hours or your extracurricular activities or reduce the number of units you are taking.

Making up a weekly schedule, you will find, is easy and fun. But sticking to it will be a challenge. The key is to make a serious commitment to your study time. I'm sure you take your class time as a serious commitment. If, for example, five minutes before class a friend asked you to go to the student union, you would say "Sorry, I'd like to but I have a class." But what about your study time? What if the same friend came up to you just as you were about to go to the library to study? I would encourage you to make the same commitment to your scheduled study time as you do to your class time. After all, much more learning occurs out of class than in class. Why are students so willing to negotiate away their study time? Every time you put off an hour of studying you are borrowing time from the future, time that will not be there.

To monitor yourself, outline the hours you actually study in red on your schedule. At the end of each week, compare your actual study hours to planned study hours for each course you are taking. If you are doing poorly in your classes, I'll bet you will see a direct correlation between your grade and the amount of studying you are doing.

Initially, you may find that you have made a schedule that you are unable to follow. Don't worry about that. In time, you will learn about what you can and cannot do and will become more proficient at scheduling your time.

Preparing For and Taking Tests

As was pointed out in Chapter 1, an important aspect of success in business study is to become a *master* at preparing for and taking tests. The best thing you can do to prepare for tests is to adopt the approaches discussed in the previous three sections. When I hear a student boast that he or she stayed up all night studying for a test, I know this is a student who is not doing well. Cramming for tests is the wrong approach. After all, if this approach worked, professors would just give all your work in one class session and test you in the next session! If you "take it as it comes," preparing for a test will merely involve scheduling time over several days prior to the test to review the material. You shouldn't have to cover new material when preparing for a test.

There is one major difference between doing homework and taking a test—time pressure. I would suggest that when preparing for a test, you spend a portion of your time working problems under a time limit. If you can, obtain tests from previous terms or, better yet, construct your own exams. Creating and taking your own practice exams will give you invaluable experience in solving problems under pressure, plus it will give you the added advantage of learning to "scope out" tests. In time you will significantly improve your ability to both work under pressure and to predict what will be on tests.

Be sure to get a good night of sleep prior to a test. Arrive at the site of the test early so that you have ample time to gather your thoughts, and be sure you have whatever materials you'll need: paper, pencils, calculator.

A certain amount of "psyching yourself up," similar to what an athlete does prior to a big game might be helpful. However, you don't want to get so nervous that you can't concentrate.

You should also try to find out whether your professor plans to grade on a "curve." If so, your absolute score is not as important as how you score relative to the class average. It may take a score of 90 to get an *A* on one test, while on another test 50 may be an *A*. Knowing that you do not need to achieve a perfect score will relieve your pretest anxiety and greatly affect the way you approach the test.

When you are given the test, don't start work immediately. First read over the entire test. Try to judge which are the easier problems and which are the harder ones. Once you have sized up the test, don't start with the first problem, start with the easiest one. As you work the easiest problems and accumulate points, your confidence will build and you will develop a certain momentum. Often easier problems contain clues or steps that will help you solve the more complex problems. Maintain some awareness of time. By dividing the time available by the total number of problems, you will know how much time to spend on each. Try to complete a problem before leaving it, and avoid jumping from problem to problem since you'll waste time getting restarted

Be sure to check your work carefully, as careless mistakes can be very costly. It may be smarter to work three of five problems perfectly than to do all five carelessly. Never leave a test early. Where do you have to go that is more important than achieving the highest possible score on that test? If you have extra time, check and recheck. No matter how many times you proofread a term paper, mistakes can still be overlooked. The same is true for a test.

By using this process of sizing-up a test, you can estimate which problems you can answer with confidence and thus predict your percentage score. In fact, jot down your estimate so that you can compare it later with the actual outcome. Over time you will become adept at sizing up tests and in the process reduce apprehension.

Summary

The purpose of this chapter was to present strategies and approaches that will enhance your academic success. The importance of setting goals so that you have a clear idea of what you are striving to accomplish was discussed. Your primary goal should be to graduate with your business degree. This is a relatively long-term goal and achieving it will require you to set many short-term and intermediate-term goals along the way.

Next, various aspects of your life situation that can interfere with your ability to reach your goal were presented. Your challenge is to balance your course load, workload, and social and family commitments so that you have adequate time and energy to devote to your studies.

In Chapter 1, we learned that to be a successful student requires that you **study hard** and **study smart**. In this chapter, we presented the most important strategies and approaches that would be put into practice by a student who wanted to **study smart**. These include making effective use of campus resources including your fellow students and your professors, and putting good study habits and study skills into practice.

The importance of making effective use of your peers through the sharing of information and engaging in collaborative learning and group study was discussed. Through these practices, you will be well prepared for the business "work world" where teamwork and leadership are valued, you will learn more, and you will enjoy it more.

The important contribution that faculty can make to the quality of your education both through their role as your classroom teacher as well as through other roles was discussed. Faculty can provide you with valuable one-on-one instruction; give you academic, career, and personal advice; provide you with leads on employment opportunities and serve as a reference; and involve you in their research activity. Approaches for building positive and supportive relationships with faculty were presented.

Finally, study skills that are critically important to academic success were presented. Perhaps most important is the idea of studying from class to class rather than from test to test. Keeping up in your classes requires a commitment to managing your time. Since test taking is such an important part of the education process, approaches for preparing for and taking tests were described.

Many of the strategies and approaches presented in this chapter may require you to make changes in both your actions and your attitudes. The next chapter on **Personal Development** will present a *Student Success Model* which will provide you a framework to understand that change process. Once you make the changes called for in this chapter, your academic performance is sure to improve.

References

1. Landis, Raymond B, *Studying Engineering: A Road Map to a Rewarding Career*, Discovery Press, 1995.

2. Smith, Karl A., "Cooperation in the College Classroom," Notes prepared by Karl A. Smith, Department of Civil Engineering, University of Minnesota, Minneapolis, MN, 1993.

3. Deming, W. Edwards, *The New Economics for Industry, Government, Education*, MIT Center for Advanced Study, Cambridge, MA, 1993.

4. Light, Richard J., *The Harvard Assessment Seminars: Second Report*, Harvard University, Cambridge, MA, 1992.

5. Carnegie, Dale, *How to Win Friends and Influence People*, pp. 65-66, Simon and Schuster, New York, NY, 1936.

Exercises

1. Establish a grade goal for each of your courses this semester or quarter. Calculate your estimated term GPA. Compare this to your current cumulative GPA. Do they match? Do you want them to match?

2. Make a list of factors that are interfering with your ability to perform academically up to your full potential. How many of these are external to you (e.g., job, family, friends)? How many are internal (e.g., lack of motivation, poor study habits, etc.)? Which of these "interferences" can you reduce or eliminate completely? Develop a plan to do so.

3. Make a list of behaviors that would send signals to your professors that you don't think their specialty is either interesting or important. Do you engage in any of these behaviors? Which ones?

4. Explain how the skills you develop in learning how to make effective use of your professors will have a direct carry over in the business "work world."

5. Who are your best friends? Are they business majors? How many business majors do you know by name? What percentage of the

students in your key business classes do you know? How could you get to know more of them?

6. If you studied for 100 hours, how many of those hours would be spent studying alone and how many would be spent studying with at least one other student?

7. If your answer to Problem 6 was that you spend most of your time studying alone, seek out a study partner in one of your key classes. Get together for a study session. Write down what worked well and what didn't work well.

8. Using the form presented at the end of this chapter, schedule your time for one week. Attempt to follow the schedule. Describe what happened.

9. Do you think that grading is objective or subjective? Ask your professors how they go about making up their final grades. Ask them what factors they consider in deciding borderline grades (e.g., *A/B, B/C, C/D*). Are these factors objective or subjective?

10. Go see one of your professors during his or her office hours. Ask one or more of the following questions:

   a) Why did you choose an academic career rather than a career in business or industry? Would you recommend an academic career to others?

   b) Would you advise me to continue my business education past the bachelor's degree? What are the advantages of getting an M.S. or MBA degree? A Ph.D. degree?

   c) I understand that your specialty is in the field of _____. How did you get interested in that field? Do you think it would be a good field for me to consider?

   d) What do you think are the most important factors in a student's academic success?

11. Make up five additional questions like the ones above that you could ask one of your professors. Pick the one you like the best and ask it of one of your other professors.

12. Pick two of the following offices on your campus. Stop by and seek information about the services offered there. (Please note that the specific names will vary from campus to campus)

a) Learning Assistance Center
b) Student Health Center
c) Counseling Center
d) Career Planning and Placement Office
e) Financial Aid Office

13 Go to your campus library and locate a book on study skills. Check out the book and scan through it. Identify several interesting sections and read them thoroughly. Write an essay on why you picked the topics you did and what you learned about them.

14 Complete the *Academic Success Skills Survey* at the end of this chapter. Based on the following point scale

Strongly agree	+2
Agree	+1
Neutral	0
Disagree	-1
Strongly disagree	-2

assign a point value or "weight" to each question. Compute your average score for the fourteen statements in the survey? Would you rate yourself as: Outstanding? Good? Fair? Poor? in practicing good academic success skills?

15 Pick six of the fourteen areas included in the *Academic Success Skills Survey* that you think are the most important for academic success. What is your average score for these?

16 From the six academic success skills you identified as most important in Problem 15, pick the two skills you feel you most need to improve. Develop an action plan for what you could do specifically to improve in each of these two areas. Implement the plan!

	MONDAY	TUESDAY	WEDNESDAY	THURSDAY	FRIDAY	SATURDAY	SUNDAY
8-9							
9-10							
10-11							
11-12							
12-1							
1-2							
2-3							
3-4							
4-5							
5-6							
6-7							
7-8							
8-9							
9-10							

ACADEMIC SUCCESS SKILLS SURVEY

1. I interact regularly with my professors positively and with benefit, both in the classroom and outside of it.

☐   ☐   ☐   ☐   ☐

STRONGLY   AGREE   NEUTRAL   DISAGREE   STRONGLY
AGREE   DISAGREE

2. I make effective use of my peers by frequent sharing of information and regularly engaging in group study and collaborative learning.

☐   ☐   ☐   ☐   ☐

STRONGLY   AGREE   NEUTRAL   DISAGREE   STRONGLY
AGREE   DISAGREE

3. I schedule my time and utilize time management principles.

☐   ☐   ☐   ☐   ☐

STRONGLY   AGREE   NEUTRAL   DISAGREE   STRONGLY
AGREE   DISAGREE

4. I devote an appropriate amount of time and effort to my studies.

☐   ☐   ☐   ☐   ☐

STRONGLY   AGREE   NEUTRAL   DISAGREE   STRONGLY
AGREE   DISAGREE

5. I keep up in my classes by mastering the material presented in the last class meeting before the next class meeting.

☐   ☐   ☐   ☐   ☐

STRONGLY   AGREE   NEUTRAL   DISAGREE   STRONGLY
AGREE   DISAGREE

6. I am aware of the importance of being immersed in the academic environment of the institution and spend as much time on campus as possible.

☐   ☐   ☐   ☐   ☐

STRONGLY   AGREE   NEUTRAL   DISAGREE   STRONGLY
AGREE   DISAGREE

7. I am aware of and practice good study skills in areas such as note taking, preparing for and taking tests, etc.

☐　　　　　☐　　　　　☐　　　　　☐　　　　　　☐

STRONGLY　　AGREE　　NEUTRAL　　DISAGREE　　STRONGLY
AGREE　　　　　　　　　　　　　　　　　　　　DISAGREE

8. I recognize the importance of goal setting and I have clear academic goals.

☐　　　　　☐　　　　　☐　　　　　☐　　　　　　☐

STRONGLY　　AGREE　　NEUTRAL　　DISAGREE　　STRONGLY
AGREE　　　　　　　　　　　　　　　　　　　　DISAGREE

9. I am effectively managing the various aspects of my personal life including interaction with family and friends, personal finances, outside workload, etc.

☐　　　　　☐　　　　　☐　　　　　☐　　　　　　☐

STRONGLY　　AGREE　　NEUTRAL　　DISAGREE　　STRONGLY
AGREE　　　　　　　　　　　　　　　　　　　　DISAGREE

10. I am highly motivated through a clear understanding of the rewards and opportunities graduating in my chosen major will bring to my life.

☐　　　　　☐　　　　　☐　　　　　☐　　　　　　☐

STRONGLY　　AGREE　　NEUTRAL　　DISAGREE　　STRONGLY
AGREE　　　　　　　　　　　　　　　　　　　　DISAGREE

11. At my university, I know other students in my classes and feel part of an academic learning community.

☐　　　　　☐　　　　　☐　　　　　☐　　　　　　☐

STRONGLY　　AGREE　　NEUTRAL　　DISAGREE　　STRONGLY
AGREE　　　　　　　　　　　　　　　　　　　　DISAGREE

12. I am aware of and make optimal use of campus resources such as the writing center, counseling center, student health center, library, and career planning and placement office.

☐   ☐   ☐   ☐   ☐

STRONGLY   AGREE   NEUTRAL   DISAGREE   STRONGLY
AGREE   DISAGREE

13. I feel good about myself and about my situation, and I am confident about my ability to succeed academically.

☐   ☐   ☐   ☐   ☐

STRONGLY   AGREE   NEUTRAL   DISAGREE   STRONGLY
AGREE   DISAGREE

14. I feel good about my institution and about the educational experience I am receiving. I would encourage others to attend the institution.

☐   ☐   ☐   ☐   ☐

STRONGLY   AGREE   NEUTRAL   DISAGREE   STRONGLY
AGREE   DISAGREE

Chapter 3
PERSONAL DEVELOPMENT

Introduction

Your success as a student and as a business professional will depend to a great extent on your development as a person.

First, we will discuss the process of **personal development** and change. Change is a natural process that you can understand through a *Student Success Model* that will be presented. We will also examine the catalysts that will help you to bring about behavioral and attitudinal changes essential to your success in business study.

Next, we will discuss two frameworks that can aid you in the important task of understanding yourself. **Maslow's Hierarchy of Needs Theory** will give you an understanding of the five fundamental human needs for motivation. Special emphasis will be placed on the subject of self-esteem and its relationship to both your level of achievement and your happiness. The second framework we will discuss is the **Myers-Briggs Type Indicator (MBTI)** which characterizes differences in people's personality styles. This will lead us into the subject of how people prefer to learn.

We will also address the important topic of **understanding others**. Understanding others is, in large measure, an extension of the process of understanding yourself. Your success as a student and as a business professional will depend on your ability to work with people who are different from you—not only people having different personality types and thinking preferences but also people who differ ethnically, culturally, and in gender.

Next, we will discuss the importance of **personal assessment**—a process that enables you to identify your strengths and weaknesses. Establishing a personal development plan that addresses your areas of weakness can maximize your personal development during your college years. Two important areas for personal development—**communication skills** and **mental and physical wellness**—will then be discussed in detail.

Finally, you will be exposed to several **motivational messages** that can assist you in clarifying your commitment to success in college.

3.1 Personal Development—Change is a Natural Process

I always ask my *Principles of Management* class: "How many of you want to change something about yourself?" I usually get blank looks from my students.

I think this natural defensiveness to the idea of change comes from the view that, if we admit we want to change, we are admitting that there is something wrong with us. This is a very counterproductive attitude. It is, however, an attitude that has been pervasive in the United States—one that was a contributing factor in our losing our #1 position in the world economy. While other countries such as Japan, Korea, Taiwan, and Germany have been striving for "continuous improvement," we in the U.S. were satisfied with the status quo. Our motto for a long time was

If it ain't broke, don't fix it.

More recently, U.S. industry has adopted the *Total Quality Management* (*TQM*) system to regain our international competitiveness. As part of your business education, you will be exposed to TQM concepts. At the heart of TQM is the philosophy that, no matter how good we are, we should be striving to improve our *quality* continuously.

The first step in implementing TQM is to determine what we mean by *quality*. This requires us to identify our "customer" and to determine what the customer wants. Next, we establish measures of our performance (*metrics*) in meeting the needs of the customer. Finally, we develop a plan for improving our performance. Ideally, this plan would involve extensive participation by people at all levels in an organization.

Total Quality Management And You

I hope that I can persuade you to adopt a **personal TQM philosophy**. You may want to view yourself as your customer, or someone else such as your parents or your spouse if you are married, or your future employer. The key point is that you strive to change (improve, develop) yourself continuously in every area which impacts your effectiveness (productivity, happiness). Your motto should be

Even if it ain't broke, improve it.

Consider, for example, a major league baseball player who is batting .315. This person was a star in high school, a star in college, and is a superstar in the major leagues. He makes $4 million a year. Yet he is still working two hours a day with the batting coach trying to raise his average to .320. In fact, the reason that he is hitting .315 is because he wasn't satisfied when he was hitting .295. The basic message is that people who are successful are those who are constantly striving to change, develop, grow, and improve.

Student development leads to academic maturity

When I use the term *student development*, I am referring to the process of developing *academic maturity*. I have a specific concept for change in mind. As a student, you have established a major life goal of completing your bachelor's degree in business that may include a specific grade point average. To accomplish this goal, you will have to "grow" academically much like when you grow emotionally or physically.

Once you have set a major life goal, you begin to place value judgments on the things you do (**your actions**), the attitudes you hold (**your thoughts**), and the feelings you have (**your feelings**). For example, we define *productive actions* as actions that support or move you closer to your goal. Conversely, *non-productive actions* are actions that tend to move you away from reaching your goal.

Similarly, we would define *positive thoughts* as thoughts that would cause you to take productive actions; whereas, *negative thoughts* are thoughts that would cause you to take non-productive actions.

Following this line of reasoning, we can speak of *positive feelings* and *negative feelings*. *Positive feelings* are those that produce positive thoughts which in turn produce productive actions. *Negative feelings* are those that produce negative thoughts that in turn lead to non-productive actions.

Examples of negative thoughts and the resulting non-productive actions are given in the following table:

Negative thought	Non-productive action
I'm so far behind, I don't get anything out of my professor's lectures.	Cut class.
I learn better studying by myself.	Spend 100% of your study time studying alone.
Accounting is too hard. I just can't do it.	Procrastinate. Put off studying.
Professors don't seem to want to help me. They make me feel stupid.	Avoid seeking help from professors outside of class.
I don't like having my life run by a schedule.	Waste time by not scheduling your time.
I don't have time for student organizations.	Avoid participation in student organizations.
I'm not good at writing and don't like doing it.	Avoid opportunities to develop writing skills.

A *Student Success Model* is shown on the next page. As indicated, achieving your goal requires that you change your actions from non-productive actions to productive actions, your thoughts from negative thoughts to positive thoughts, and your feelings from negative feelings to positive feelings. Through these changes, you will "develop" as a student. There are two fundamentally different approaches for bringing about the change: 1) behavior modification; and 2) counseling (therapy).

Behavior Modification as a Process for Change

The basic premise of *behavior modification* is that you choose your actions. So if you are choosing non-productive actions, you have complete freedom to change and choose productive actions.

You have less control over your thoughts. You cannot help having negative thoughts. However, you can become more "conscious" of the negative thoughts you do have and when you detect them you can try to change them to positive thoughts. Generally, changing a negative thought to a positive thought can be accomplished by finding a higher context for your thinking. Often your goal can provide that higher context for your thinking.

STUDENT SUCCESS MODEL

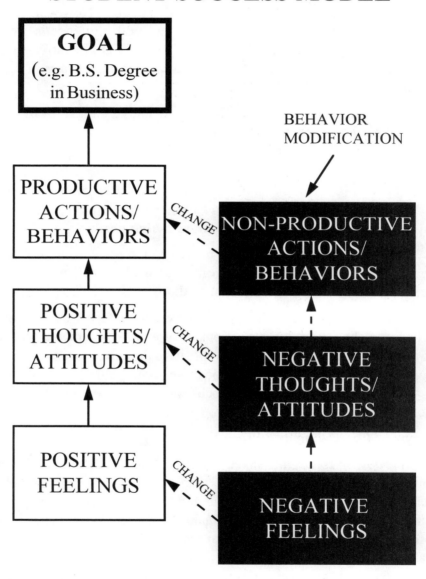

Consider the following example. Since you have a test coming up in your marketing class, a productive action would be to study marketing from 7:00 p.m. - 10:00 p.m. tonight. Behavior modification would hold that you have the total capability to choose that action. However, you may be having thoughts such as "I'd rather go out with my friends"; or "I'm tired and don't feel like studying tonight." These are negative thoughts because, if acted on, they will lead you to a non-productive action (i.e., not studying).

Your challenge is to identify such negative thoughts and try to change them. For example, the thought that

"I don't feel like studying tonight"

can be changed to

"I really do want to study tonight because I want to do well in my marketing class so I can achieve a high grade."

So as you see, changing negative thoughts can usually be accomplished by looking at them from your goal—whether it is a short-term, intermediate-term, or long-term goal.

You have much less direct control over your feelings. However, if you begin to choose productive actions in support of a personal goal and if you work to change your thoughts to positive thoughts in support of those actions, in time you will feel more positive about yourself and about your life. How you feel about yourself (self-esteem) is an extremely important factor in the quality of your life.

Therapy or Counseling as a Process for Change

Therapy or *counseling* takes a different approach to bringing about change in your actions, thoughts, and feelings. Whereas, behavior modification comes down from the top of the actions, thoughts, and feelings process illustrated in the *Student Success Model*, therapy comes up from the bottom. The basic premise of therapy is that you have negative feelings that are the result of childhood traumas and that these negative feelings cause you to have negative thoughts that in turn produce non-productive actions.

Consider the following example:

> *Jane R. gets terrible feelings of anxiety whenever she faces the necessity to make a presentation in front of other people. She has thoughts like "I'm a lousy public speaker." When she performs the action, she gets so nervous that she does a poor job. Finally, out of desperation she goes for counseling. During therapy, she recalls that when she was in elementary school her teacher criticized her for doing a poor job of reading aloud in front of the class. This experience left her traumatized. As an adult, she is able to re-examine that experience and realize that it was okay for a third grader to make a mistake and that her teacher was not really trying to ruin her life. She is able to forgive herself and forgive her teacher. By diffusing the negative feelings, she begins to develop the thought that "Maybe I can do a good job of speaking in public." And she does!*

Although therapy/counseling is an excellent way to accelerate your personal development and bring about positive change, it may not be accessible to you because of the cost. Some free counseling may be available on your campus, but generally not enough to bring about significant results.

I hope this discussion has increased your receptivity to change and that you have made a commitment to choose those *productive actions* that will lead you to success in business study. One step in choosing productive actions is to change any negative thoughts you are having. You can begin right now. If you are having the thought "This won't work for me," try changing it to: "I'm going to try this. It could work!"

3.2 Catalysts for Change

Sounds easy. Just change those negative thoughts to positive ones; start choosing productive actions; and everything will be just great. Actually, you will find that making productive change is not as easy as you would think. Changing your behavior requires you to successfully navigate three steps. You can choose to either use each of these steps as a catalyst for change or you can choose to let each of them serve as a barrier to change. The choice is up to you.

1) Knowledge
2) Commitment
3) Action

Knowledge

By *knowledge*, we mean that:

You know what to do.

One of the main purposes of this book is to provide you with the knowledge of those strategies and approaches that will enhance your effectiveness as a student. Much of that knowledge was presented in Chapter 2. Hopefully, you have studied Chapter 2 thoroughly and recognize that implementation of many of the strategies and approaches presented there will require you to change your behavior. Some examples of this change are presented below:

Non-Productive Action	Productive Action
CHANGE	
Neglect studying $\longrightarrow$	Devote significant time and energy to studying
Delay studying until test is announced $\longrightarrow$	Master the material presented in each class prior to next class
Study 100% alone $\longrightarrow$	Study collaboratively with other students
Avoid professors $\longrightarrow$	Interact regularly with professors outside the classroom

Avoid participation in $\longrightarrow$ Participate actively in student student organizations organizations

Gaining the knowledge presented in Chapter 2 does not guarantee change. A prime example of where new knowledge does not produce change is with regard to smoking cigarettes. When I was growing up, people simply did not know that smoking caused cancer. Today, no one can deny knowing that it does. The relationship between smoking and lung cancer is an example of a new knowledge base. But many people still smoke. They have failed to change because they did not make a commitment to act on the new knowledge.

Commitment

By *commitment*, we mean that you not only know what to do but that

You want to do it.

Developing that commitment requires you to go through the process of examining each academic success strategy and deciding whether you want to put it into practice. Do I want to schedule my time? Do I want to study from class to class rather than from test to test? Do I want to study collaboratively with other students? Do I want to make effective use of my professors? Do I want to spend more time on campus? Do I believe these are strategies and approaches that will enhance my academic success?

A commitment to doing something is really a thought. The process of making a commitment to the new knowledge base involves making a change in your thoughts. And changing your thoughts is an important first step in changing your actions. As an example, changing your thought from "I don't have anyone to study with" to "I'm going to try to find a study partner" is a key first step in the process of changing your behavior from solitary study to collaborative study.

Action

Commitment to the knowledge does not guarantee a change in one's actions. The final stage is action or implementation. By *action*, we mean that you not only know what to do and want to do it, but that

---

You do it!

Many people who smoke want to stop in the worst way. They may, in fact, have stopped smoking many times. There are many reasons why you may fail to make changes in your behavior that you know you should—in effect, to work against yourself. For example, let's assume that you are not putting sufficient effort into studying and are doing poorly in your classes. How can this be? You want to be successful in school. You want to get all of the rewards that a business career will bring to you. Still, you are not doing what is required for success.

One of the primary reasons you may not be willing to change is that there may be a payoff for you to keep doing what you are doing. You have adopted your current behavior patterns because they satisfy some need or want that you have.

**Changing to new behaviors will require you to give up
old behaviors, ones that you may like very much.**

For example, you may go home or to your residence hall as soon as you get out of class. You may do this because you get a great deal of pleasure from the distractions you find there such as friends, family, TV, stereo, food in the refrigerator, and telephone. Choosing to stay on campus to study with other students, to seek help from professors, or to use the resources of the library may be less enjoyable to you. You may have to really work on yourself to change your thought from "I enjoy going home" to: "If I go home, it's likely that I won't study. I'm going to stay at school until I get my work done."

There are other reasons why you might choose non-productive behaviors. Human psychology is very complicated and doesn't always make sense. You may be "afraid" to study because if you do and still fail, it will reflect on your ability. Or you may be trapped in a "victim" role, preferring to blame your failure on factors or people external to yourself. Perhaps you feel you were forced to go to college by your parents. By not studying you are showing them that you are your own person; that you are not going to do what they want you to do.

> *Making change is the act of accepting responsibility for your actions and to begin to view yourself as the creator of your life.*

3.3 Self-Analysis: A Starting Point

Understanding yourself is a key aspect of becoming a productive and happy person. There are other payoffs as well. As you grow in your understanding of yourself, you will grow in your ability to understand other people.

Understanding yourself is a lifelong process. Human beings are very complex. As a result there are many different models or frameworks available to describe human behavior and human psychology.

Some of these frameworks are more useful than others. In fact, some are not even valid. I always wonder how I am supposed to believe that one-twelfth of the people in the world (all those born under my zodiac sign) have something in common with me. Others are over-generalizations. For example, there is a book on the importance of birth order [1]. If you are the first born, based on this book, you would be reliable, conscientious, driven to succeed, serious, self-reliant, well organized, and on and on. This is an example of a framework that tries to put all people into one of three categories (i.e., firstborn, middle child, and last-born)—an obvious oversimplification.

We will focus on two frameworks that I think can be particularly useful to you as a student.

The first framework is Maslow's Hierarchy of Needs [2]. This will provide you with an understanding of those needs that must be met if you are to be motivated to succeed in your studies. One of these needs is the need to feel good about yourself. Because your self-esteem is a very important factor in your productivity and in your happiness, we will address it is some detail.

The second framework we will address is the Myers-Briggs Type Indicator (MBTI), which can help you to identify your personality type and relate this information to the typical teaching style of business school professors.

Maslow's Hierarchy of Needs

Motivation is an inner drive or impulse that causes you to act in a certain way. Maslow [2] clarified the relationship between motivation and unmet needs. In his theory of motivation, which has become widely accepted, Maslow put forth a hierarchy of needs as shown below.

MASLOW'S HIERARCHY OF NEEDS

According to Maslow's theory, *needs* must be satisfied from the bottom up. If a lower level need exists, you will become highly motivated to satisfy that need. When lower needs are satisfied, higher level needs become important, and you become motivated to satisfy those needs.

It is important to distinguish between *needs* and *wants*. *Needs* are things that you must have, things that are essential. *Wants* are things that you desire but do not have to have. For example, you may want to have a car for transportation, but having one may not be essential, especially if public transportation would meet your basic need of transportation. Don't let unnecessary wants distract you from academic success.

At the lowest level are your physiological needs for food, water, air, and shelter. Hopefully, you are satisfying these needs. If not, it is unlikely that you will be able to focus on your academic work.

At the <u>second level</u> are your safety needs including the need for security and for freedom from fear of physical and psychological threats. Again, I hope that these needs are satisfied for you. If you are afraid of a bully on your hall or of a former boyfriend, it is doubtful that you will be able to devote adequate concentration to studying.

At the <u>third</u> level are your social needs such as needing to belong, to be accepted, and to receive affections and support from others. These social needs are generally met by family or by friends. If you left home to go away to school, you may be experiencing a period in which your social needs are not being met. You have left your family and old friends and have not yet established new relationships. It is important for you to develop new friends. Otherwise, unmet social needs can interfere with your studies. Fortunately, many of your classmates are also looking to make new friends.

At the <u>fourth</u> level are your needs for esteem including self-respect, achievement, and recognition has been identified. You need to feel good about yourself and to feel as though you have the respect and appreciation of others. We will address the important topic of self-esteem in the next section. Gaining appreciation from others, including your professors and other students, will be related not only to your academic success but also how you treat other people. In a later section, we will discuss keys to effective interpersonal communication.

At the <u>fifth</u> and highest level is your need for self-actualization. *Self-actualization* is the full development of your ability and ambitions. It is the need you have to reach your highest potential, or put in simple terms "to do your best." This is the need that causes you to want to excel on a test, to do your best in a game of chess, to learn, to grow, and to develop. Perhaps best put by Maslow [2]:

> *Even if all these needs are satisfied, we may still often expect that a new discontent and restlessness will soon develop, unless the individual is doing what he or she, individually, is fitted for. Musicians must make music, artists must paint, poets must write if they are to ultimately be at peace with themselves. What humans can be, they must be. They must be true to their own nature. This need we may call self-actualization.*

Obviously, to be a successful student, you must be motivated and able to pursue your need for self-actualization. This means that you must first satisfy your physiological, safety, social, and esteem needs. Perhaps the most challenging of these are your esteem needs.

Satisfying Your Need for Self-esteem

As indicated by Maslow's Hierarchy of Needs, self-esteem is a fundamental human need. We cannot be indifferent to the way we feel about ourselves. *Self-esteem* is a critically important factor to virtually every aspect of our life. It influences what we choose to do, how we treat others, and whether we are happy or not.

Many problems faced by our society such as drug and alcohol abuse, crime and violence, poverty and welfare abuse, teenage pregnancy, the disintegration of the family, and the high dropout rate among high school students are directly related to the low self-esteem of many of our citizens. As an example the California Legislature recently established a Task Force to Promote Self-esteem to make recommendations on what the State can do to enhance the self-esteem of its citizens. The Task Force defined *self-esteem* as:

> *Appreciating my own worth and importance and having the character to be accountable for myself and to act responsibly toward others.* [3]

According to Nathaniel Branden [4], self-esteem is made up of two interrelated components: *self-efficacy* and *self-respect*. Self-efficacy is your sense of competence. Self-respect is your sense of personal worth.

To be self-efficacious is to feel capable of producing a desired result. Self-efficacy is related to your confidence in the functioning of your mind and in your ability to think, understand, learn, and make decisions.

Self-respect comes from feeling positive about your right to live and to be happy, from feeling that you are worthy of the rewards of your actions, and that you deserve the respect of others.

It is important to have both self-efficacy and self-respect. If you feel competent but not worthy, you may accomplish a great deal, but you will lack the capacity to enjoy it. You may feel that you must continually prove your worth through achievement. Overachievers and "workaholics" are generally striving to meet their need for self-respect by feeling competent and productive.

There is a strong correlation between our self-esteem and our behaviors. According to Branden [4], healthy self-esteem correlates with:

Rationality
Realism
Intuitiveness
Creativity
Independence
Flexibility
Ability to manage change
Willingness to admit mistakes
Benevolence
Cooperativeness

Poor self-esteem correlates with:

Irrationality
Blindness to reality
Rigidity
Fear of the new and unfamiliar
Inappropriate conformity
Rebelliousness
Defensiveness
Overcontrolling behavior
Fear of others
Hostility toward others

It is no surprise that research [5] has found that high self-esteem is one of the best predictors of personal happiness. The value of self-esteem is not merely that it allows you to feel better, but also that a healthy self-esteem will be a key factor in your productivity and success. According to Branden [4]:

> *High self-esteem seeks the challenge and stimulation of worthwhile and demanding goals. Reaching such goals nurtures self-esteem. Low self-esteem seeks the safety of the familiar and undemanding. Confining one's self to the familiar and undemanding serves to weaken self-esteem.*

How can you enhance your self-esteem? The continuous feedback loop between your actions and your self-esteem described by Branden points the direction. The level of your self-esteem influences how you act. Conversely, how you act influences the level of your self-esteem.

Recall the *Student Success Model* presented in Section 3.1. As we discussed there, you **choose** your actions. You can choose productive actions or you can choose non-productive actions. You have less control over your thoughts, but you can catch negative thoughts and work at changing them to positive thoughts. Behavior modification tells you that if you choose productive actions in support of a personal goal and you work at changing your thoughts to positive thoughts in support of those actions, in time your feelings will change. You will feel better about yourself and your life. **Your self-esteem will improve**.

> *Your college years provide a unique opportunity for you to enhance your self-esteem by building both your self-efficacy and your self-respect.*

Your business education will increase your knowledge and develop your thinking skills, your communications skills, and your ability to work with others. All of this will increase your confidence in your ability to face life's challenges and to achieve whatever goals you set for yourself. Through this process, you will build your self-efficacy.

You will have many opportunities to build your self-respect and your feeling of personal worth as well. Academic success will bring positive feedback from your professors and from your fellow students. More tangible rewards such as scholarships, internships, and admission to graduate school can be yours. You can be president of a business honor society, be the team leader of your institution's entry in a national student case competition, be paid to work on a professor's research project, or co-author a paper which is presented at an international conference. These accomplishments will be respected by others and will enhance your sense of self-worth.

Success in business study will enhance both your feeling of being competent and your self-respect. These together will build a healthy self-esteem. But it is up to you. You can let the negative feelings associated with low self-esteem produce negative thoughts that lead you to non-productive actions and failure. Or you can choose productive actions and positive thoughts that will lead you to success and to feeling good about yourself and your life.

Myers-Briggs Type Indicator (MBTI)

Individuals are different. We each have a preference for how we interact with the world around us, how we learn and how we make decisions. The famous Swiss psychologist Carl Jung did the seminal work on psychological types [6]. Jung's work led to the Myers-Briggs Type Indicator (MBTI) which is widely used today [7]. The MBTI characterizes individuals in four areas:

1) Does the person's interest flow mainly to:	
The outer world of actions, objects, and persons?	E-extrovert
The inner world of concepts and ideas?	I-introvert
2) Does the person prefer to perceive:	
The immediate, real, practical facts of experience and life?	S-sensing
The possibilities, relationships, and meanings of experiences?	N-intuiting

3) Does the person prefer to make judgments or decisions:	
Objectively, impersonally, considering causes of events and where decisions may lead?	T-thinking
Subjectively and personally, weighing values of choices and how they matter to others?	F-feeling
4) Does the person prefer mostly to live:	
In a decisive, planned, and orderly way, aiming to regulate and control events?	J-Judging
In a spontaneous, flexible way, aiming to understand life and adapt to it?	P-Perceiving

I would encourage you to seek out the opportunity to take the MBTI. It is very likely that the test is administered somewhere on your campus—most likely the testing office, the counseling office, or the career planning and placement office.

Taking the Myers-Briggs will enhance your understanding of yourself. The end result is that you will find out that you are one of sixteen types based on combinations of four pairs of letters (E or I, S or N, T or F, P or J).

I must admit I always have trouble with instruments that determine psychological types. A question like "Would you rather read a book or go to a party?" is really difficult for me. Sometimes I would prefer to read a book and other times I would prefer to go to a party. If I answer that I'd rather go to a party, the results will say I'm an extrovert. If I answer that I'd rather read a book, the results will say I'm an introvert. This reflects one of the main problems with the MBTI. You are typed as being either one way or the other. There is no way to indicate as to whether the preference is strong or weak.

This does not mean the MBTI is of no value, but rather you should use it as one of many tools to help you understand yourself and appreciate differences in others.

The Business World Needs all Types

I'm sure by now you're asking the question "How can your understanding of the MBTI benefit you as an business student?" There are three primary ways.

- First, understanding that people are different and that the differences are not only okay but also desirable can **assist you both in appreciating your own uniqueness and also in appreciating the uniqueness of others.**

- Second, your personality type and thinking preferences define your learning styles and these styles may not coincide with the teaching styles characteristic of your business professors. If this is the case, it is important that you **understand how to create your own learning experience to meet your needs.**

- Third, as we will discuss in Chapter 5, the business profession encompasses a wide variety of different job functions. Knowing your thinking preferences *may* guide you in **selecting a job function for which you are most suited.**

I often hear from students that their professor does not understand them or they have been advised to avoid a professor because he or she is difficult. Other students come into my office and relate stories of a brilliant teacher and mentor. Both sets of students are talking about the same professor. I will give you the same advice I give to my students. In both college and in your professional life, you will work for and with all kinds of personality types. When possible, you will naturally choose a personality type best suited to your needs. However there may not always be a choice available to you. Accepting this can allow you to overcome these differences and focus on the job at hand. Would the college experience be better if all professors and students took the MBTI and you were able to schedule a "personality match" for every class? Not really. Learning to work effectively with people who are different from you is excellent preparation for what you will face in the business work world.

You Create Your Learning Experience

So what if your personality type is "introverted" or you prefer to make judgements subjectively? Can you learn if the way you are being taught does not match your primary learning style? The answer is emphatically yes! You are primarily responsible for creating your learning experience. Most of the learning takes place when you study the material either by yourself or collaboratively with other students.

> **What you must do is make sure that the way you study is compatible with your preferred learning style.**

If you are a "perceiving" (MBTI) thinker, you are most likely a visual learner and need to create visual presentations of the information you are learning. If your professor is concentrating primarily on the details, you need to establish the "big picture" and the context for the material you are learning. Think about how the topics you are studying relate to future trends. Try to broaden your "single answer" problems to open-ended problems and solve those problems. You will probably enjoy case study courses most and excel in them. Look for ways to express your artistic ability and creativity by, for example, taking an art class.

If you are a "feeling" (MBTI) thinker, you will most likely have a strong preference for collaborative learning. Organize study groups and assist the students in the groups in developing their teamwork skills. Look for opportunities to participate in group projects. Become active in student organizations. Volunteer to tutor or mentor a fellow student or seek employment as a tutor or peer counselor through many of the formal student service programs the university operates. Look for ways to define how the material you are studying impacts people. Find ways to meet your needs for personal expression by, for example, taking an acting class, music lessons, or participating on a sports team.

3.4 Understanding Others/Respecting Differences

One of the most important areas in which you can strive for personal growth and development is in respecting people who are different from you. Business, now more than ever, is a team-oriented profession. Your success both as a student and as a business professional will be closely related to your ability to interact effectively with others. As a professional, you will be required to work with, manage, and be managed by people differing from you in personality styles and thinking preferences and in gender, ethnicity, or cultural background.

Ethnic and Gender Differences

Among the critically important areas of difference are gender and ethnic differences. As an example twenty years ago, 73 percent of business graduates in the U.S. were males. This is no longer the case. The percentage of women among business graduates has been increasing steadily. As indicated by the chart below, over forty-eight percent of 1994/95 business graduates were women.

1994/95 Business Graduates by Gender
Reference: U.S. Department of Education 1997[8]

	Number	Percentage
Men	121,898	52%
Women	112,425	48%
TOTAL	234,323	100%

The next chart depicts the change in percentages of business graduates from different ethnic groups between 1986/87 and 1994/95.

Change in Business Graduates by Ethnicity from 1986/87 to 1994/95
Reference: U.S. Department of Education 1997 [8]

	1986/87	1994/95
African Americans	6.1%	8.7%
Hispanics	2.6%	4.6%
Native Americans	0.3%	0.4%
Asian Americans	2.5%	5.6%
Foreign Nationals	3.4%	5.4%
TOTAL	**14.9%**	**24.7%**

As indicated, roughly 25% of current business graduates are ethnic minorities and foreign nationals. This percentage has almost doubled over the past decade and is expected to continue to grow in the future.

Unfortunately, prejudice, bigotry, and discrimination continue to be prevalent in our society. We seem to have a compulsive need to build ourselves up by putting others down.

How we treat others is closely related to our self-esteem. If you don't feel good about yourself, it is likely that you won't feel good about others. The converse is well stated in the report of the California Task Force to Promote Self-Esteem [3].

> *The more we appreciate our own worth and importance, the more we are able to recognize and appreciate the worth and importance of others as well.*

We now live in a multi-ethnic, multi-cultural society. The old *melting pot* idea is no longer operative. As a nation, we are now more like a "stew," or a mixture of separate and different peoples, each having its own unique characteristics. The concept of a *melting pot* has become offensive. Why should I strive to be the same as you? The quality of my life and the contributions I make are related to my special qualities and my uniqueness as an individual. If I come from a different background and experience than you, I can do things and think about things in ways that you cannot.

As a student and a future professional, it is important that you learn to respect and value people from different ethnic backgrounds than yours. This may require you to work through certain prejudices that you have.

A Personal Story

I grew up in a totally white midwestern environment. At the time I completed high school in 1967, there were no minorities in my hometown, and I did not understand nor was I introduced to the issues of racism. I had not personally witnessed racial discrimination. Everyone I knew just applied for opportunities and was successful based on their qualifications. Certainly with that kind of upbringing, I was naive My first exposure to racial issues came after I joined the Air Force and was required to attend "race relations" classes.

> *This was the one of the most enlightening experiences of my life. I heard the stories of discrimination from African Americans, Hispanics, Latinos, women and a number of other minority groups. Although the people in my class were in my unit and I had been working side-by-side with them, I had no awareness this was their life experience.*
>
> *After one of these classes I had a long talk with one my best friends, who happened to be an African American, and I asked him point blank if he thought I was guilty of any discriminatory practices. He looked at me and said, "You are the most racist friend I have." I was completely floored. He laughed, and further explained: "You try too hard not to be racist and therefore treat me differently from your other friends. Just treat me like everyone else no better no worse."*
>
> *I learned a lot from my friend, and this is probably why I believe so strongly in our college Diversity Program. There must be an avenue for communication. We can read and study about inequality but only when the problem becomes real to you will become involved in the solution.*

As we discussed in Section 2.2, knowledge <u>can</u> produce change. Sensitivities can develop by understanding the injustices that are around us. I am deeply involved with my College of Business Administration Diversity Program. We define diversity as celebrating the similarities as opposed to identifying the differences. I recommend you read the book *Proversity* by Lawrence Otis Graham [9]. We use this book in our diversity courses and it was a valuable resource as we established the goals and objectives of our program.

We did not have a program at the time I was hired. I attended conferences on ethnicity and visited universities and colleges to study and understand minority student programs. We built a composite diversity program that incorporated the best ideas. We met with groups of students (minority, non-minority, business and non-business students) to get their perspectives. It is sometimes very disheartening to hear students say if "that" group would just make the effort to join our study group or have lunch with us or play with us we would welcome them. The common perspective is "it is not my responsibility to take the initiative, let them start." As a society we must move beyond this and become leaders not followers. The first step in this process is to recognize and deal with any societal barriers.

Stereotyping is Unnecessary and Unfair

One of the primary issues related to prejudice is *stereotyping*.

> **A *stereotype* is a fixed conception of a person or a group which allows for no individuality.**

Business students are often stereotyped as *capitalists* who care only about making money and have no interest in or skill for dealing with people unless there is a financial return. The obvious problem with stereotyping a group is that the stereotypes don't apply to all individuals in the group.

Just as I'm sure you would not like to be automatically labeled as a *capitalist* merely because you are a business student, I hope you will refrain from stereotyping others. The best way to approach people who differ from you in ethnicity or gender is to suspend judgment. Take the view that all things are possible. Resist the need to make up things about someone you don't even know.

Stereotyping can lead to such unfair and inequitable results. Sheila Widnall, Secretary of the Air Force in the Clinton Administration, wrote a powerful paper several years ago [10] outlining many of the obstacles experienced by women. According to Dr. Widnall:

> *Studies of objective evaluations of the potential and the accomplishments of women give quite discouraging results. Such studies in which male or female names are applied to resumes, proposals, and papers that are then evaluated by both male and female evaluators consistently show that the potential and accomplishments of women are undervalued by both men and women, relative to the same documents with a male attribution.*

I hope that you will agree that we have a long way to go in providing equal and fair treatment to all people.

Improving Your Effectiveness in Cross Cultural Communications

What can you do to improve your effectiveness in working with and communicating with people who differ from you? I would encourage you to seek out opportunities to interact with people from different ethnic and cultural backgrounds than yours. You can learn a great deal from them and improve your interpersonal communication skills in the process. If you really want to grow in this area, take a course in cross-cultural communications. I think you will find the subject very interesting and you will develop skills that will be useful throughout your life.

As a nation, we have come a very long way in the area of race relations and multi-culturalism. Professor Robert Cottrol of Rutgers Law School gives us optimism for the future [11].

Perhaps our most important contribution to the twenty-first century will be to demonstrate that people from different races, cultures, and ethnic backgrounds can live side by side; retain their uniqueness; and, yet, over time form a new common culture. That has been the American story. It is a history that has much to tell the world.

I hope you will contribute to making this vision a reality!

3.5 Assessment of Your Strengths and Weaknesses

If you are committed to personal development, growth, and change, a good starting point is to do an assessment of your strengths and weaknesses. Recall in Chapter 1, we presented four models or frameworks for viewing your education. These models provide an excellent basis for personal assessment.

The AASCB Model indicated those skills and/or attributes that you should gain from your business education. A personal assessment based on this model would involve evaluating how strong you are with regard to each of the following attributes:

Assessment Based on AACSB Attributes Model

High ethical standards
Understanding of the perspectives for global/international issues
Understand the influence of political, social, legal and regulatory, environmental and technical issues
Understand the impact of demographic diversity on organizations
A foundation knowledge of business in Accounting, Behavioral Sciences, Economics, Mathematics and Statistics
An appropriate foundation in written and oral communication
The ability to use library and computing facilities

You could choose to do a personal assessment based on the Academic Model. This model identified the factors the business program at the University of Notre Dame strives to impart to its students. Better yet, find out if your institution has its own list of such attributes.

Assessment Based on an Academic Model

Provide a sound liberal arts education to include appreciation for scholarship, innovation and ethical behavior
Recognition of the importance of administration, management and entrepreneurship and recognition of the responsibility to manage resources in a manner that will contribute to both organizational and societal goals
Inspire students to be leaders in their profession
Facilitate the integration of the students' professional expertise with the Notre Dames' sense of values

Similarly, you could do a personal assessment based on the Employment Model. This model identifies those factors employers may use in evaluating you when you apply for a job.

Assessment Based on Employment Model

Real-world work experience
Technical skills
Academic degree and grade point average
Leadership qualities
Personal presentation
Attitude
Communication skills
Problem analysis and analytical thinking
Adaptability, drive and initiative
Preparation for the interview
Career interest

Or you could do a personal assessment based on Astin's Student Involvement Model. This model outlines key metrics for measuring the quality of your education as reflected by your level of "student involvement."

Assessment Based on Astin's Student Involvement Model

Time and energy devoted to studying
Time spent on campus
Participation in student organizations
Interaction with faculty members
Interaction with other students

How would you go about doing this personal assessment? The assessment process would simply involve rating yourself (e.g., on a scale of 0 to 10; 10 being highest) on each item listed. For example, on a scale of 0 to 10 how would you rate your ability to work with other people? How would you rate your effectiveness in using your professors? How would you rate your computer skills?

For those items for which you give yourself a high mark, just keep on doing what you are doing. We have a tendency to seek out areas in which we are strong. For example, if we have strong computer skills, we spend lots of time on the computer. As a result, our strengths are naturally reinforced. What we need to do is work on our weaknesses by creating a personal development plan.

Personal Development Plan

We tend to avoid areas in which we are weak. For example, if we do not write well, we avoid classes that require writing. If we are shy, we avoid people. *Avoidance behavior* ensures that the areas in which we are weak will stay weak or even get progressively weaker.

You probably can't take on all of your weaknesses at one time. You will need to prioritize them in order of importance and choose several of the most important for action. For each area chosen, develop a *personal development plan*. What are you going to do in the next week? In the next month? In the next year?

As an example, if you are shy and lack good interpersonal communication skills, your plan might include some or all of the following action items:

1)   Talk more with people

2)   Discuss your problem with a counselor in the counseling center

3)   Take a course in interpersonal communications

4)   Read a book on self-esteem

5)   Join the campus Toastmasters Club

6)   Take an acting class

7)   Join a student organization.

The time you are in college is the time to work on your areas of weakness. You can make mistakes there and the price will be low. If you avoid dealing with your areas of weakness, they will follow you into your business career.

> ## There, the price for failure will be much higher!

3.6 Developing Your Communication Skills

A key area for your personal development is the area of communication skills. We will place a particular emphasis on this topic because the progress you make will be in large part up to you. Although you will receive a certain amount of training through your formal education process, it is very likely to fall short of what you really need.

The Importance of Communication Skills

Communication skills are the lifelines of any organization. Corporations are aware of their importance and they emphasize the need for students to acquire communication skills prior to coming into the business world. Here are just a few comments for reference.

John H. Bryan, CEO and Chairman of the Board of Sara Lee Corporation, underscoring his belief that communication skills are critical in career advancement, states:

> *"If I were designing a business school, communication would be the most important course in the curriculum."* [12]

According to Andrew Drysdale, Communications Director, Boise Cascade Corporation:

> *"Business communication affects a company's bottom line directly and indirectly. Done well, communication helps us to avoid costs and make the most of opportunities. Anyone can enhance his or her business career by demonstrating the communication skills that are necessary for business and business people to succeed. Take time to master these skills and make them an important part of what you to offer to an employer."* [13]

Lee Iacocca, former CEO of the Chrysler Corporation, says:

"Don't ever use the word charisma, because I don't know what it means. If it means you communicate better than other people that's what everybody should try to do. You must, no matter what you are running, communicate effectively with your constituencies." [14]

Increasing the emphasis on communication skills in business education is a current objective of the Business Advisory Council (a group of business executives who support business education) for my institution. The Council has supported the establishment of a Business Communication Center. We recognize the need to teach business communication classes to our students. Thus our response to the question "If the business curricula were revised or increased, how would you prioritize the need for additional instruction?" is

> *More instruction in written and oral communications.*

Developing communication skills is a MUST for successful business professionals. Although your knowledge of business principles and your ability to solve problems are certainly important, their greatest value will come through your effectiveness in communicating your knowledge and ideas to others.

In this section, we will overview the kinds and purposes of communications that business professionals typically engage in, and suggest ways for you to prepare for the communication demands you will face after graduation. First, though, you need to understand the fundamental role of communications: why they are such an important part of your education.

Consider the following scenarios:

- As a result of your senior marketing class, you come up with an entrepreneurial business plan, which will produce the next generation of personal communication devices—two-way audio/visual cellular phones. You now want to patent, produce, and market the device.

- During a summer internship at a major financial institution, you are assigned to a team of financial analysts who are researching the next multimillion-dollar acquisition of the company. After two months of preparation, the team is ready to make its recommendations to the Board of Directors.

- With your business diploma in hand, you are finally ready to step out on your own and start your first full time career job. You have narrowed your selection to three possibilities: a bank, an investment firm, and a manufacturing firm.

At stake in each of these scenarios is your ability to communicate— both orally and in writing. To patent, produce, and market a new product will involve written correspondence with all kinds of individuals, groups, and organizations—from the U.S. Patent Office to prospective buyers. It will also involve numerous kinds of oral communications—from one-on-one telephone calls to major sales presentations. As a member of the financial analysis team at the financial institution, you will most likely take part in either writing the analysis or presenting the findings to the Board of Directors. And, of course, landing a job after graduation will depend largely on both your written communications (cover letters and resume) and oral communications (telephone calls, interviews, and possibly short presentations).

You see, no matter what you do, effective writing and speaking are integral parts of the job. Here's why. Your business education combined with your creativity and common sense, are what can lead to new ideas and new business opportunities. But turning any new idea of yours into a successful business venture involves a process that relies mostly on your communication skills. That is, you need to be able to "sell" your ideas to others, convincing them that your idea is worthy of their time and investment. And this holds true whether you work for yourself or for a major business or industry.

It's a good time to pause in your reading at this point to reflect on your own communication skills. Some business students are gifted with an ability to write clearly and speak persuasively without any noticeable effort. Many, however, tend to shy away from speaking and writing because they don't feel confident about their skills in these areas.

For such students—and you may be one of them—the problem is usually just a lack of practice. As the newest member of the Microsoft Corporation programming team, you might suddenly be handed a lap top computer and told "check this out and make sure the new operating system is bug free. Bill Gates will be giving an international presentation and you are to ensure that he doesn't have any problems." I'm sure you would be quite apprehensive. Wouldn't you try to beg out, or at least find a substitute—someone who knew more about the operating system than you do?

The same is true for communication skills. If you haven't done much writing or speaking, you're like the novice computer programmer who may know a great deal about programming, but who just can't put them all together very well at this time. Does the novice computer programmer lack ability? Probably not. Similarly, if you're a novice communicator, you don't lack aptitude. You just need to PRACTICE, PRACTICE, PRACTICE. And if you're reading this book as a first year college student, the news is good.

> *You have four or five years to develop*
> *your skills as a master communicator!*

Whether you're the rare student who can speak and write effortlessly, or the more common student who struggles with writing and speaking, the key word for you is PRACTICE. Lots of practice, particularly under the guidance of someone that can point out and correct weaknesses, will do wonders to help. But practice alone is not enough, and what you practice will differ according to the particular skill you want to strengthen.

In the remaining sections on Communications Skills, we'll examine the two mainstays of communications—writing and speaking—and suggest ways for you to develop yourself in each area.

Written Communications

More than once, I have had former students come me up to me and remark about the lack of communication skills they possessed at the time of graduation· They admitted during their college years they were skeptical about the need to develop their writing skills and that they tended to avoid intensive writing opportunities. When they began their careers, they had quickly "seen the light." Their reason for coming up to me years later was to call my attention to what they felt was an omission in the curriculum. The graduates strongly recommended a required business communications course for all business students which stressed quality writing.

Quality in writing is a difficult concept to define and measure, but my former students are right. Quality is an important feature of writing. Employers are always complaining about "poor quality" writing skills of new college hires. When pressed about what they mean, however, they give a variety of responses. Mostly, they combine all quality problems into the category of "bad grammar," even though they usually mean something else—like spelling, punctuation, diction, or sentence structure. They also use "quality" to refer to the <u>look</u> of the written document. Does its appearance reflect the work of a professional? Is it word-processed? Is it centered on the page? Is there enough white space so that the text doesn't look cluttered?

However you define quality—the text's professional appearance, its mechanical correctness, or a combination of both—it sends a tremendously important message about you, the writer. Contrary to how it looks, writing is never just a one-way communication. Whenever you write something to someone else, your reputation—your "ethos"—is being tested.

Consider, for example, two versions of the same memo. Which of the following memo writers would you rather do business with? That is, which writer presents a more attractive ethos?

Memo "A"

TO: Mary Phillips

FROM:Bradely Harrington

Send me 8 key boards for the Micoteeh computer model 4a659782.

The paertnumber is aasl6789. Creit my account for the units I ahve returend. They were the wrong parts. If you ahve any questions concerning billing refer to my contract

Memo "B"

TO: Mary Phillips, Sales Representative

From: Bradley Harrington, Techno Products LTD.

Mary, please send eight keyboards for the MicroTec computer model number 4A659782. The part number is AASl6789. The computers arrived with the standard keyboards instead of the new "Quiet Touch" keyboard. I returned the standard keyboards yesterday.

I do not believe there is a difference in price. But if we owe anything, just bill our account. The account number is B4532.

Thanks for your assistance.

The answer is fairly obvious, isn't it? The quality of Memo *B* outshines the quality of Memo *A* in a number of ways. The writer of Memo *B* has taken care to spell words correctly; to write clear, simple sentences; to project a sense of professionalism; and even to impart a tone of good will. We can't say the same about the writer of Memo *A*.

Whether you're writing a 30-page investment analysis or just a short progress report, the quality of your work will depend on your ability to present complex information in a structured, thorough, and understandable way.

The best way to ensure quality in your written work is to follow the guidelines outlined earlier in this chapter regarding Total Quality Management (TQM). The first step—determine what *quality* means—we have already done. Quality writing is derived from the text's content, correctness, and appearance. Content—what the text says and how it is organized—depends on the second step in the TQM process: identifying the customers (or readers, in this case) and determining their needs.

This is probably the most crucial, and often the most problematic, step. It is crucial because your intended reader(s) will dictate the tone and style of your writing, as well as the complexity and arrangement of information. To illustrate the importance of *audience* read the following anecdote.

> A foreign-born plumber in New York City wrote to the Federal Bureau of Standards that he had found that hydrochloric acid did a good job of cleaning out clogged drains.
>
> The Bureau wrote back to him:
>
> *"Though the efficiency of hydrochloric acid is indisputable, the corrosive residue is incompatible with metallic permanence.*
>
> The plumber replied he was glad the Bureau agreed.
>
> Again the Bureau wrote:
>
> *"We cannot assume responsibility of the production of toxic and noxious residue resulting from the employment of hydrochloric acid and suggest you use an alternative procedure."*
>
> The plumber replied again that he was happy the Bureau agreed with his idea. Finally the Bureau wrote:
>
> *"Don't use hydrochloric acid. It eats the hell out of the pipes."*

Do you see how audience governs content to a great extent? You could, I'm sure, come up with numerous other examples of how different audiences would affect the content of any report or memo. But what about a situation in which the readers of a particular text have varying levels of technical knowledge? This kind of situation, which happens quite frequently, can really complicate your writing process. Read the following anecdote.

> WASHINGTON (AP) - Every weekday afternoon at 4 p.m., after the stock markets have closed, the Pentagon releases a list of contracts awarded that day by the various services.
>
> The announcements are normally brief and frequently unfathomable to those unfamiliar with military acronyms and code words. Occasionally, though, a contracting officer will decide the reader deserves a better explanation to what's being purchased - with mixed results.
>
> The following single sentence was contained in a contract listing Thursday disclosing an award to the Westinghouse Electric Co.

> *"Westinghouse is being awarded a $3,317,467 firm fixed price completion contract to design, develop, fabricate and test an advanced development model to demonstrate the techniques to maintain pulse-to-pulse stability in a tactical radar transmitter at levels necessary to support adequate moving target indicator performance to counter validated threat scenarios while operation with widely varying pulse widths and repetition rates to facilitate power management."*
>
> Translation*:*
>
> **The Air Force is trying to develop a new radar and needs a more sophisticated transmitter to power it.**

This article was in a local newspaper and as you can guess it was taken out of context. The original author never intended the memo for the general public, but rather for highly sophisticated technical personnel. However it proves the point that once you put something in writing it becomes the standard by which you are evaluated.

The diagram below shows the "rainbow" of possible audiences that you will need to consider whenever you have something to write.

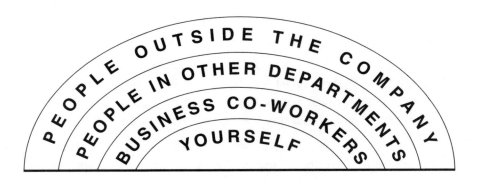

AUDIENCE "RAINBOW"

If the writer's audience stays within the bands closest to the center, the writing task is relatively easy. But as the audience spreads to the outer bands of the rainbow, the writing task can become increasingly difficult. Why? Because the writer has to explain complex concepts in language understandable to a non-technical audience. And, unless you're writing the most basic of memos, it is likely that your reports, proposals, and other written documents will be read by people from all "spectrums" of the audience rainbow.

In determining your audience, you also need to address the next step in the TQM process: determining what the "customer" (or audience) wants. Ask yourself, "What is the purpose of this report, letter, proposal, or even school assignment?" Nadler and Hibino, creators of the highly effective *Breakthrough Thinking* problem-solving method [15], recommend that, no matter what your task, you should develop a *purpose hierarchy* before attempting to complete your writing task. You start such a hierarchy by asking the question above (i.e., "What is the purpose of the report . . . ?"), and then posing the same question repeatedly to each response. Here's an example:

Q. What is the purpose of writing the acquisition financial analysis report?

A. To justify the financial feasibility of the proposed acquisition.

Q. What is the purpose of that?

A. To convince the Board of Directors to approve the acquisition.

Q. What is the purpose of that?

A. To help the company grow.

Q. What is the purpose of that?

A. To ensure the company's financial health.

And so on. Nadler and Hibino say that while *purpose hierarchies* can be practically endless, they are important in that they help you see a problem—or, in this case, a writing task—globally. Even though you eventually settle on <u>one</u> purpose in the hierarchy you devise for any writing task, the others, especially those higher on the hierarchy, help guide what you write.

You'll see, too, that purpose hierarchies take you through most or all of the bands on the "audience rainbow" shown above—even for the simplest of documents.

What starts, then, as a relatively pro-forma, internal document, sent from one person to another, gains significance—and the possibility of multiple audiences—as it is put through a purpose hierarchy.

In summary, you never write in a vacuum. Indeed, the context in which you write is often more complex than it might initially appear. And, in all cases, one's writing is bound to reflect on the writer, with the quality of the written text (content, correctness, and appearance) helping to shape the ethos of the person who writes it.

Developing Your Writing Skills.

If I've convinced you of the importance of good writing skills, the ball is now in your court to do something about strengthening them. Because you cannot expect to improve your writing skills overnight, or even in a semester's time, you've got to start TODAY.

What should you do? As I mentioned earlier, the key to better writing (and all communication skills) is **practice**. To get yourself to practice, take all the writing courses you can—not just those required by your college or university. Find courses in disciplines across the curriculum that involve extensive writing. When faced with a writing assignment, do it early so that you can get feedback from your instructor or a writing tutor, and then rewrite it based on their suggestions.

Beyond formal coursework, look for opportunities to write. Keep a journal. Write letters to friends and family. Write a poem or a short story. Volunteer to write an article for the campus newspaper. Write a critique of this book and send it to me.

Above all, read—anything and everything. Research in language development has shown that reading is a significant way to build writing skills. Read the newspaper, magazines, technical journals, and novels. Set goals for your reading, particularly during break periods. Take the time you would normally watch television and use it for recreational reading.

Developing Your Oral Communications Skills

If business people do a lot of writing, they do <u>more</u> speaking: one-on-one, in meetings, through formal presentations. In some respects, speaking may seem easier than writing. Since talking to people is a normal, frequent part of everyday life, you surely must be skilled and comfortable doing it. Right? Not necessarily. In fact, certain speaking situations—like having to address a large audience—are often so traumatic that people typically rank public speaking as one of their most frightening experiences.

The reason why public speaking can be so terrifying is no mystery. It has to do with the nature of oral communication itself and its difference from written communication. That is, the spoken word is a "one-shot deal." Once a word is uttered, you can't go back and change it. Writing, on the other hand, is a bit more hidden. Before making a document public, you can revise and revise until it's perfect.

Your audience also tends to weigh more heavily in speaking than in writing. In writing, your audience is essentially imagined, unreal, while in speaking your audience is right in front of you. In a sense, speaking becomes a performance that you give to your audience, and, like the ballet dancer or tightrope walker, one wrong step and the performance is ruined. If your ethos is at stake when you write, then it's <u>really</u> put to the test when you speak before others.

The immediacy of the audience and the "one-shot" nature of the spoken word cause much of the anxiety associated with public speaking. But the smart speaker uses these "negatives" to his or her advantage. If executed well, a talk can be your most effective communication tool. You will have the opportunity to command the attention of important people. And there's no better way to sell your ideas than through a spirited, persuasive presentation. Would you rather read a 50-page, single-spaced report about the financial status of the company's latest acquisition, or listen to a short presentation on it?

How do you give an effective presentation? And how do you channel "stage fright" in positive ways? Answering these questions fully would take too long. Indeed, books have been written on each subject. I only want to alert you to the multiple demands of oral communications and to encourage you to start developing your oral communication skills NOW.

In general, we can divide oral communications into three kinds of speaking situations:

1. Interpersonal communications, in which you and one person converse;

2. Group communications, in which you speak either as the leader of or participant in a small group; and

3. Formal presentations, in which you, either alone or with others, address a large audience.

Interpersonal communications may strike you as the easiest, and you're probably right. We all spend good portions of our days talking one-on-one with others, especially since the advent of the telephone. Still, effective interpersonal communications involves knowledge and skills that you need to have—such as listening techniques, and sensitivity to and understanding of cultural differences. Probably most critical is what Stephen R. Covey [16] calls the "principles of empathic understanding," which he summarizes in the adage:

> ### *Seek first to understand, then to be understood.*

This advice might seem obvious or self-evident, but believe me, it can be very difficult to put into practice. For we all develop biases and prejudices and so we risk closing ourselves off to new and possibly better ideas. But if we make it a point to first understand what someone else says—if we learn to resist jumping to conclusions and listen openly, seeing the world the way the other person sees it—we open ourselves to all kinds of possibilities. We also create bonds with the other person that last far beyond any temporary exchange of ideas. For, as Covey points out, to empathize with others fills one of the most vital human needs besides physical survival, and that is psychological survival—"to be understood, to be affirmed, to be validated, to be appreciated." I would urge you to read what Covey has to say about empathic understanding in Chapter 5 of his best-selling book *The Seven Habits of Highly Effective People* [16]. I guarantee it will help you in all facets of your life, not just your career.

Group communications involve the same skills and concerns of interpersonal communications, but in more complex ways. For purposes of this discussion, we'll define a "group" as any gathering of three or more people who are assigned to some project or task, ongoing or temporary. In this sense, a group could be a standing committee charged to develop and oversee a company's hiring policies, a special project team assembled to develop a marketing plan, or even a study group that you and your fellow students form to prepare for an upcoming exam. Sometimes you will be in charge of the group, which entails leadership and initiative on your part.

But whether you lead or merely participate in a group, you need to learn the three C's of effective group dynamics:

> *Collaboration*
>
> *Consensus*
>
> *Compromise*

That is, you need to be able to work together (*collaboration*) in a democratic process that relies on the shared views and goals of all members (*consensus*) and often entails subjugating your personal agenda for the betterment of the group (*compromise*).

Formal presentations, in which you speak directly to an audience for an extended period of time, generally do not involve the "give and take" that interpersonal and group communications do. As noted earlier, presentations are more like a performance than other communication scenarios, so the demands are somewhat different. Rather than needing to listen empathetically or work to achieve a consensus, you need to engage your audience and sustain their focus and attention—which is no easy trick. If you are a first year student, chances are you haven't had to give many formal presentations. But you've probably had to listen to a lot, so you know how deadly that can be! Just think of some of the lectures you've had to sit through. I'm sure you've found yourself more than once in the position of the man in the cartoon on the following page.

The strategies and techniques of effective presentations are numerous—too numerous to detail here. However, since formal presentations figure centrally in your success, and since public speaking skills are only developed over time, I want to address a few of them.

REAL LIFE ADVENTURES by Gary Wise and Lance Aldrich

**Many times, the body language of the audience
will tell you how your presentation's going.**

REAL LIFE ADVENTURES © GarLanco. Reprinted with permission of
UNIVERSAL PRESS SYNDICATE

As with writing, it is extremely important for you to assess your audience and purpose. That is, to <u>whom</u> are you speaking and <u>why</u>? Carefully answering these two questions alone can make the difference between a successful presentation and a mediocre one. In determining your audience, use the same guidelines that we discussed for writing. Pay close attention to the audience rainbow, particularly the needs, expectations, and limits of "non-technical" people. Put yourself in <u>their</u> shoes when deciding what to say and how to say it. In determining the content and structure of your presentation, construct a purpose hierarchy first. Settle on <u>one</u> purpose to inform your talk, but keep in mind all the other purposes as well, especially those higher on the hierarchy.

When discussing written communications, we stressed <u>quality</u> as an important feature, and we defined quality as a combination of appropriate content, grammatical correctness, and professional appearance. When you make formal presentations, slightly different quality metrics apply. Content, of course, continues to be an important consideration and, as we noted above, depends largely on your audience and purpose—just as it does in writing. The grammatical "correctness" of your speech is also somewhat important, but not nearly so important as your overall <u>delivery</u>. By delivery I mean the way you present your ideas and the impact you have on your audience. Generally, you can test the effectiveness of your delivery by asking yourself:

- Do I make my main message or point clear?

- Do I infuse my presentation with energy? Am I animated and focused when I talk?

- Do I balance my focus on content with an equal focus on audience?

- If I switched places with my audience, would my attention and interest be maintained?

In summary, whether you're making a formal presentation, working with others in a group setting, or just talking with a colleague, one thing is certain: you will rely heavily on your oral and interpersonal communication skills. And, as with writing, these skills take time to develop, so you need to start working on them now.

Developing Your Oral Communication Skills.

There are lots of opportunities to develop your oral communication skills while you are in college. One of the best and most obvious is to take courses. A speech communications course will introduce you to the field of rhetoric and give you practice in the rhetorical "modes of discourse" (i.e., describing, informing, analyzing, persuading, and so on). Psychology courses will teach you the principles of human relations, group dynamics, and cross-cultural communications. An acting course will give you instruction and practice in effective delivery.

Extracurricular activities can also be helpful. Getting involved in business student organizations or school athletic programs will go far in building your interpersonal and teamwork skills. Running for student offices and holding positions in the student body government will hone your public speaking and presentation skills.

There are even excellent opportunities beyond the college campus for developing your oral communication skills. With the growing availability of camcorders, for example, you can arrange to have yourself videotaped and then judge for yourself how well you make a presentation or collaborate with others. You might also consider joining professional organizations, like Toastmasters, that are devoted exclusively to developing public speaking skills.

Pursue whatever avenue appeals the most to you. What's important is that you **DO SOMETHING** and **START TODAY.**

3.7 Mental and Physical Wellness

To be productive and happy, it is important that you take care of yourself personally. With the rigors and demands of being a student, it is easy to ignore your emotional and physical well being. But that is a big mistake! Tending to your personal needs is a must.

Many people are not aware of the interrelationship between our physical and emotional health. The fact is they are strongly interrelated: our physical well being greatly affects our emotional state—and vice versa. For example, one of the best remedies for emotional stress is vigorous physical exercise. And I'm sure you've noticed that when you are mentally "up," you tend to feel good physically, whereas if you're emotionally down, you often feel physically fatigued or even get sick.

<u>Keys to Good Health</u>

Since each of us is so unique and our emotional and physical states so complicated, this section is only meant to point out a few ideas for your consideration. Most obviously and most importantly, to expect a high level of mental and physical health, it is essential that you:

- **Eat nutritionally**
- **Engage in regular aerobic exercise**
- **Get adequate sleep**
- **Avoid drugs**

What you eat significantly affects your physical and mental state. A proper diet consists of fresh fruits and vegetables, lean meat in moderation, and whole grain products. Avoid processed foods, fatty foods, and sugar. Not only will you feel better now, but you'll also reduce your chances of heart attack, cancer, and other diseases later.

Regular aerobic exercise in which you get your heart rate above 130 beats per minute for more than 20 minutes at least three times a week is essential to good physical condition. If you're not already engaged in some form of exercise, you should consider taking up brisk walking, jogging, swimming, biking, rowing, aerobic dancing, or any vigorous activity that will improve your physical fitness and that you do regularly.

Different people require different amounts of sleep and the amount needed may change as you grow older. Only you can determine how much sleep you need. Just remember that your work efficiency will decrease if you are getting either less or more sleep than you need.

Drugs are abundant in our society. Some, such as caffeine, alcohol, and nicotine, are legal; others, such as marijuana and cocaine, are illegal. Regardless of their legality, all can be harmful and my advice to you is simple: avoid them. Not only do drugs detract from your physical and mental health, they also can greatly interfere with your ability to study.

Balancing Work and Play

One important aspect of your mental state is the **balance you strike between immediate and future gratification.** By seeking too much immediate gratification and therefore not getting your work done, you are likely to feel guilty. You'll probably then worry about the fact that you are not studying, putting yourself in a mental state in which you cannot study.

On the other hand if you work too much, too long, or too hard, you begin to feel deprived. Feelings of deprivation and resentment can begin to sabotage your commitment. You may begin to doubt whether the sacrifice is worth it.

What you need to find is a proper balance between work and play. One approach is to tie work and play together through a system of rewards. Rewards can be small things, like taking a break, going for a walk, watching your favorite TV show, taking an hour for recreational reading. Or they could be larger things, such as going to a party, buying yourself some new clothes, or going away for the weekend with a friend. The point is that, rather than take the view that the work you are doing will not have a payoff until far into the future, you provide yourself with frequent and immediate rewards for your hard work.

Managing Stress

The term *stress* was borrowed from engineering by Dr. Hans Selye [17], an early pioneer in the area of stress management. Selye defined stress as "the response of the body to any demand made upon it to adapt, whether that demand produces pleasure or pain."

Stress can be externally imposed or internally imposed. Certainly, the announcement by three of your professors that each has scheduled their mid-term exam on the same day can create stress for you. Causes of internally imposed stress include unmet expectations, high personal standards, irrational ideas, and other demands you place on yourself.

Stress can be either positive or negative. *Eustress* is a positive form of stress that motivates individuals to attain higher levels of performance. The "butterflies" an athlete experiences before the big game can produce inspired play. *Distress* is the negative form of stress. It can distract you from being the best that you can be. It can debilitate and be devastating to physical and mental health.

Some common causes of stress include worry, frustration, anxiety, and depression. Frustration is our response to being prevented from gratifying certain impulses or desires. For example, it would be frustrating if you were unable to enroll in the accounting course you need as prerequisite for a future course. Worry and anxiety are closely related. Both are your response to a perceived threat. Anxiety is a somewhat stronger emotion. You become worried if your roommate fails to come home for several days. You become anxious when you develop pains in your chest. Depression is an extreme form of worry and is an emotional condition characterized by feelings of hopelessness and inadequacy. You can become depressed if your fiancée breaks up with you, if you fail your statistics course, or if you have been arrested for drunken driving.

Each of these emotions is a potential source of stress (stressor). Stressors do not affect everyone in the same way. What would cause stress for one person may not even bother another. Your reaction to stressors is undoubtedly related to your self-esteem. If you feel competent and worthy, you are in a good position to handle stress. An individual's experience of stress is related to his or her perception of lack of control. For individuals who lack self-esteem and do not feel in control of their lives, stress can produce anger, depression, and physical illness.

Whether *eustress* or *distress*, Selye [17] demonstrated that stress produces the "fight or flight" response from our body. This is an instinctive physical reaction to threat, either physical or psychological, we inherited from our ancient ancestors. Under stress, blood is diverted to the brain and muscles for clearer thinking and quicker reflexes, the heart rate accelerates, the blood pressure rises, the respiration rate increases, and the pupils of the eyes dilate. This is generally an inappropriate and unnecessary response since as a business student you will neither need to "fight" nor "flight." Modern stressors are usually symbolic, requiring no physical action.

To ensure your effectiveness as a student, it is important that you learn to cope with and manage stress. Kaplan [18] presents a list of ten quick stress dischargers that you can use to deal with short-term stress:

1.	Have a good cry.
2.	Create something manually.
3.	Talk it out.
4.	Have some fun.
5.	Take a walk.
6.	Try a massage.
7.	Take a hot bath.
8.	Breathe slower.
9.	Learn to relax.
10.	Turn to your friends.

It is important that you use strategies such as those presented above to prevent the type of "burn-out" that can come from unchecked or unresolved bottled-up anger or prolonged stress. In the long term, good nutrition, regular exercise, relaxation, and good planning and organization are keys to keeping your stress level low.

If all else fails, it is important that you seek counseling or medical treatment. Extreme stress can lead to severe physical incapacitation, even death through disease or suicide.

3.8 Motivating Yourself

Seeking to be the best you can be (self-actualization) is something in your control.

A Personal Story

Throughout my adult life, I have emphasized the value of education. I owe almost everything of quality in my life to my education. I have had so many unique and rewarding experiences, so many challenges, so many opportunities. I've been paid well to do work I enjoy. I have been able to travel, write, speak, teach, and influence others. I have gotten to know many interesting people. I have had options and choices and control over where I live and what I do. I can hardly imagine going through life without an education.

Often I wonder why I have been so fortunate. How is it that I went so far with my education? Where did my motivation come from? Actually, it is as clear as anything could be. It started with my parents who made it possible for me to go to college right out of high school. They were very insistent that I would be the first in the family to achieve a college degree. But I was young and thought I knew all the answers, I did not apply myself at first and dropped out of college to get a job. It took me about six years to recognize the wisdom of my parents. Without the college degree "doors" were closed, opportunities for advancement were non-existent and most of all I knew I was not living up to my potential. My parents never explicitly told me they were disappointed in me, but I knew.

My motivation came to me in a tri-level package—my parents, my desire for new opportunities, and my family. My only regret is that it took me six years to recognize the wisdom of my parents. I received my first degree at age 29. Doors have been opening ever since that day.

You may have been sent similar messages about the importance of education from parents, relatives, friends or co-workers. If so and you listen, you are indeed fortunate. You are very likely to succeed.

Not all students have been motivated as to the value of getting their education. I have known students, in fact, whose parents were opposed to their going to college, preferring instead that they work to help support the family.

Regardless of whether or not you were instilled with a high level of motivation, you are now an adult. You can think for yourself. You can develop your own reasons for wanting to get your education. You can motivate yourself.

We have already addressed the idea of motivating yourself through an increased awareness of the rewards and opportunities of a business career. In Chapter 5, we will discuss my "top ten list" of what it will mean to the quality of your life when you successfully complete your business degree. In the following sections, several additional perspectives are offered regarding the value of your education.

Power of Positive Thinking

You can make an analogy between jogging and going to college. People take up jogging because they perceive certain benefits. They expect to live longer, feel better, breathe easier, and lose weight. Initially they may dislike the experience of jogging, suffering through it solely for the end result. Eventually, however, most joggers learn to enjoy the experience. They come to enjoy the physical elements of jogging—the rhythmic cadences of moving and breathing, the harmony between body and mind. Joggers find that long periods of jogging can lead to particularly unique experiences; the so-called "runners' high," a heightened sensitivity to the world around them, an ability to think creatively and imaginatively.

Business students can be thought of like joggers. At first they may resent or dislike the college experience but persevere because of the future benefits they anticipate: career opportunities, money, social status, security. But they eventually come to appreciate their schooling, not only for the benefits it promises, but for the experience itself.

If, like the novice jogger, you find that you dislike school, you are not focusing on the positive aspects of being a college student. You need to recognize that you have created an attitude that may have nothing to do with reality. In fact, you probably are in the best situation of your life and just not aware of it. Surely you have heard people say that their college years were the best years of their lives. Why do you suppose they say this?

If you do have a negative attitude toward school, now is the time to change it. For it's more than likely that you are neither performing at your peak effectiveness nor enjoying what should be a most exciting, rewarding time in your life. Learn to focus on the positive aspects of being a college student. Some of the most significant of these aspects are:

__Growth Period__. As a college student, you are in an unusually heavy growth period. One indication of this is the way in which you are "outgrowing" your friends from high school who are not going to college. Probably never in your life will you be in such an intense period of learning and experiencing new things as when you are in college.

__Exposure to People__. You are in an extremely people-oriented environment. Never again will you be with so many people of the same age and interests as when you are in college. The friends you make during your college years can be important and helpful to you throughout your life.

__Manager of Your Time__. As a college student you are working for yourself. You have no boss. No one to tell you what to do. Except for your class time, you are pretty much free to manage your time and your affairs.

__Starts and Stops__. School starts and stops somewhat like the running of a race. When the race starts you put out a great deal of effort, maybe more than you would like to, but you do so because you can see that it will end. When it does end, you then have an extended period of time for rest and rejuvenation—a break you will not have once you start your business career.

When you learn to appreciate these and other unique aspects of being a college student, you will see an improvement in your academic performance. Remember that:

Positive attitudes bring positive results!

Negative attitudes bring negative results!

Summary

The purpose of this chapter was to assist you in your process of growing, changing, and developing personally. A *Student Success Model* was provided to give you an understanding of the process of your personal development and change. Having a clear picture of this model will enhance your effectiveness in choosing actions that will result in academic success. Change is not easy, so specific catalysts were identified.

A key to personal development is understanding yourself. There are many frameworks we can use to understand different aspects of human psychology and behavior. Two of these, which are particularly useful to you as a business student, were presented.

Maslow's Hierarchy of Needs was presented to help you understand what is necessary for you to be motivated to reach your full potential. A case was made for the importance of a healthy self-esteem to your success as a student and as a person. The Myers-Briggs Type Indicator was presented as a model for characterizing personality styles. The topic of understanding others and respecting differences in people was discussed. It is important that you develop your effectiveness in working with people who differ from you.

Personal assessment as a tool to identify and work on areas in which you need to improve was discussed. One critically important area is communication skills, including written and oral communications. Specific suggestions were made as to how you can work to develop your communication skills.

The relation of your physical and mental wellness to your academic performance was discussed. A particular focus was placed on the importance of managing stress. Finally, the importance of focusing on the positive aspects of being a college student was stressed.

REFERENCES

1. Lehman, K., *The Birth Order Book*, Bantam Doubleday Dell, New York, 1985.

2. Maslow, A., *Motivation and Personality*, Harper and Row, New York, 1970.

3. "Toward a State of Esteem: The Final Report of the California Task Force to Promote Self-Esteem and Personal and Social

Responsibility," California State Department of Education, Sacramento, CA, 1990.

4. Branden, Nathaniel, *The Six Pillars of Self-Esteem*, Bantam Books, 1994.

5. Myers, David.G., *The Pursuit of Happiness: who is happy—and why,"* W. Morrow, New York, NY, 1992.

6. Jung, C.G., *Psychological Types*, Princeton University Press, Princeton, NJ, 1971 (originally published in 1921).

7. Briggs, K.C. and Myers I.B., "Myers Briggs Type Indicator, Form G," Consulting Psychologists Press, Palo Alto, CA, 1977.

8. U.S. Department of Education, National Center for Education Statistics, Integrated Postsecondary Education Data System (IPEDS), "Completions" Survey, 1988 and 1997

9. Graham, Lawarence, *Proversity*, John Wiley and Sons Inc., 1997

10. Widnall, Sheila E., "AAAS Presidential Lecture: Voices from the Pipeline," *Science*, Vol. 241, pp. 1740-1745, September, 1988.

11. Cottrol, Robert, "America the Multicultural," *The American Educator,* Winter, 1990.

12. M.E. Guffey, *Business Communication*, Wadsworth Publishing Company, Belmont, CA, 1994

13. K. G. Locker, Business and *Administrative Communication*, 4th Edition, Irwin McGraw Hill, Boston, MA, 1997

14. J. Harcourt, A.C. Kringan, P. Menier, *Business Communication*, 3rd Edition, South-Western Publishing, Cincinnati, OH, 1996

15. Nadler, G. and Hibino, S., *Breakthrough Thinking: Why We Must Change the Way We Solve Problems and the Seven Principles to Achieve This*, Prima Publishing, Rocklin, CA, 1990.

16. Covey, Stephen R., *The Seven Habits of Highly Effective People*, Simon & Schuster, New York, 1989.

17. Selye, H., *Stress without Distress*, J.B. Lippincott, Philadelphia, PA, 1974.

18. Kaplan, Myron S., "Beating the Training—Stress Connection," *Data Training,* March, 1988

Exercises

1. After doing some research on "Total Quality Management," answer the following questions. How does TQM differ from management approaches you have observed in the university you attend, organizations you belong to, or companies you have worked for?

2. For the next week, write down at least five negative thoughts you are able to identify. Describe at least one non-productive action that is likely to be the result of each negative thought. Also write down a positive thought that you could substitute for the negative thought. Describe at least one productive action that is likely to result from each positive thought.

3. When we receive a stimulus (e.g., see food), we often act (e.g., eat the food) and then think (e.g., I shouldn't have eaten the food). How can we change this order (stimulus $\Rightarrow$ action $\Rightarrow$ thought) in a way that it might lead us to choose productive actions more frequently?

4. Add ten examples of productive actions (actions that will enhance your academic success) to the list of six used as examples in Section 3.2.

5. Do you think "behavior modification" can work for you? Why? Do you think "counseling/therapy" would benefit you? Why? Why not?

6. Convert the following negative thoughts to positive thoughts by finding a higher context in which to view the situation that has led to the negative thought:

   a. I wish I were taller.
   b. I'm homesick.
   c. I don't have any friends.
   d. My statistics lectures are boring.
   e. I don't know if I like business.
   f. I wish I could find a better roommate.
   g. I don't have time to exercise regularly.

7. Examine the following productive behaviors:

   a. Study collaboratively with other students.
   b. Devote significant time and energy to studying.
   c. Study from class to class rather than from test to test.
   d. Make effective use of professors outside of the classroom.
   e. Practice good time management principles.

f. Immerse yourself in the academic environment of the institution.

g. Actively participate in student organizations.

Do you:

1) Have adequate knowledge about the behavior?

2) Have you made a commitment to the behavior? If not, why not?

3) Are you implementing the behavior? If not, why not?

8. Consider Maslow's Hierarchy of Needs. How well are your needs being met at each level? Think up one or two ways to better meet your needs at each level. Do them.

9. Consider the ten items listed in Section 3.3 that correlate with healthy self-esteem. Write down a brief definition of each item. How many of the items would you use to describe yourself?

10. Based on the results of Problems 8 and 9, would you say that you have a healthy self-esteem or a poor self-esteem? Explain. What can you do to improve your self-esteem?

11. Write a paragraph describing yourself in terms of the four personality indicators which are measured through the Myers-Briggs Type Indicator (MBTI). From this analysis, what MBTI indicator (e.g., ENFP) do you think best describes you?

12. List five ways you could benefit from knowing your MBTI personality type.

13. Find out if you can take the MBTI on your campus (at the testing office, counseling center, etc.). If you can, take the test and determine your MBTI personality type. Compare the results with your response to Problem 11.

14. List five reasons why you should strive to improve your effectiveness in working with and communicating with people who are different from you.

15. Conduct a personal assessment based on the "Employment Attributes Model" by rating yourself on a scale of 0 to 10 (10 being highest) listed in Section 3.5. Identify the areas in which you rate the lowest. Develop a personal development plan to improve in each of these areas.

16. Evaluate yourself, on a scale of 0 to 10 (10 being highest), with regard to the following personal qualifications:

a. Enthusiasm
b. Initiative
c. Maturity
d. Poise
e. Ability to work with other people

What can you do to improve yourself in the areas in which you have given yourself a low evaluation?

17. Assess the quality of your education as measured by Astin's "Student Involvement Model." Give yourself a rating of 0 to 10 (10 being highest) for each of the five areas listed in Section 3.5. Develop a plan for improving in each of the areas you feel you are weak. Implement the plan.

18. List ten types of documents that you might have to write in your business career. Which of these do you feel qualified to write at this time?

19. Develop a "purposes hierarchy" for the question "Why am I studying business?" Carry this at least five to seven levels up the hierarchy. Does your result indicate that you are doing the right thing? Why?

20. Write a proposal seeking funding (e.g., from parents, private foundation, scholarship committee, etc.) to support your education. Explain how much money you need, why it's needed, and how giving you the money will ultimately benefit the *funding source*.

21. Develop a personal development plan for improving your writing skills over the next three to five years. Implement the plan.

22. Develop a personal development plan for improving your oral communication skills over the next three to five years in each of the following areas:

a. Interpersonal communications
b. Group communications
c. Formal presentations

How do your plans differ for each of these areas?

23. One strategy for improving your vocabulary is to write down words you don't know from things you read, look them up in the dictionary, and try to add them to your vocabulary. Carry this strategy out for the following words which appeared in Chapter 3:

> ethos
> empathic
> efficacy
> attribution
> rhetoric
> intuiting
> metric
> catalyst
> diversity

24. In Reference 16, Covey gives five levels at which we can listen to other people:

1. Ignoring
2. Pretending
3. Selective listening
4. Attentive listening
5. Empathic listening

Define each of these levels. As you talk with people over the next week, identify your listening level each time. Then write up a short critique of your listening skills.

25. Conduct a personal assessment based on the four keys to good health listed in Section 3.7:

a. Eat nutritionally
b. Engage in regular aerobic exercise
c. Get adequate sleep
d. Avoid drugs

Develop a personal development plan for any areas in which you rate yourself low.

26. For the next week, schedule your study time in blocks. Following each block of study time, schedule time to do something you enjoy as a reward for doing your work. At the end of the week, evaluate how this worked for you.

27. Write a paragraph describing the messages your parents sent you about the value of a college education. Do you agree with these messages?

28. In addition to the four positive aspects of being a college student discussed in Section 3.8, list five others. Do you believe the adage that "Positive attitudes bring positive results; negative attitudes bring negative results"? If you do, why? If you don't, why not?

Chapter 4
EDUCATION HAS NO LIMITS

Introduction

How do you view your education? A limited view would be that you get an education by passing a prescribed set of courses. A quality education should be much more extensive than this. This chapter will introduce you to a number of ways you can expand your education and in doing so, be significantly better prepared for a successful career.

First, we will discuss the value of participation in **student organizations** and extracurricular life. The skills you can develop through these activities could be as important to your business career as those you develop through your formal academic work.

Then we will describe opportunities for you to gain practical business experience through involvement in **business student competitions and research projects.**

Next, we will discuss strategies and approaches for seeking **pre-professional employment** including summer jobs, part-time jobs, and cooperative education work experiences. Through pre-professional employment you can gain valuable practical experience, better define your career goals, and earn money to support the cost of your education.

Finally, we will discuss opportunities for you to **put something back** into the educational system of which you are a part. Opportunities for service can range from visiting high schools to recruit students to providing feedback to faculty for their use in improving their teaching effectiveness.

4.1 Student Organizations - A Place to Learn Life Skills

In Chapter 1, we presented several models for viewing your education. Both Astin's *Student Involvement Model* and the *Employment Model* indicated that you should participate actively in student organizations and extracurricular campus life. The reasons were slightly different for each model, but very much related. The *Involvement Model* indicated that the **quality** of your education will be enhanced through participation in student organizations. The *Employment Model* identified experience in campus activities, particularly participation and leadership in extracurricular life, as an important factor used by employers in evaluating candidates for employment. Employers place a high value on such participation because of its importance in developing highly sought after leadership and organizational skills.

If you do not participate actively in a student organization, I expect you have reasons for not doing so. Perhaps you have never thought of becoming involved. Or perhaps you are not aware of the benefits of such participation. On the other hand, maybe you have considered becoming involved but decided that you don't have enough time. Or maybe you are shy and are reluctant to join a group of people you don't know.

I hope I can persuade you to let go of these or other reasons you might have. Participation in student organizations can contribute significantly to the quality of your education. Through such participation, you can meet your social needs, develop your leadership and organizational skills, engage in professional development activities, receive academic support, and participate in service activities.

Imagine yourself, as you near graduation, interviewing for a position with a company. You can bet one of the questions you will be asked by the interviewer is: "Can you give me any examples of your involvement in student organizations, particularly those in which you took on leadership roles?" How do you think it will be viewed when you answer: *"Not really. I was too busy studying."*

A word of caution: Be selective about your involvement in such activities. The opportunities to participate are so numerous that you could wind up neglecting your studies.

Your institution could have literally hundreds of student organizations. These include fraternities and sororities, recreational organizations, service organizations, ethnic and gender based organizations, academic organizations, and professional organizations.

Business Student Organizations

Of the many different student organizations, the ones that are the most accessible to you and have the greatest potential for benefit are the academic and professional student organizations that operate within your business college. Most of these business student organizations can be classified into one of three categories:

1) Department-related clubs

2) Business honor societies

3) Ethnic- and gender-based business student organizations

Department-Related Clubs. It is very likely that your college has student clubs or organizations corresponding to your business major. For example, if you are an accounting major, you could join the Accounting Association Club. As a Finance major, you would want to become involved in the Investments Fund Club, and so forth.

Other clubs or organizations may serve business students in all disciplines. For example, the Entrepreneur Club would have the purpose of fostering entrepreneurial drive in students from all business disciplines. My institution has a student organization called the Council of International Business Development Club, which promotes hands-on international business experience via coordinated international business internships. Students for Responsible Business (SRB) is an international organizational with its nonprofit center in San Francisco. With chapters in over 30 schools around the country SRB's mission is to introduce corporate social responsibility as a viable additive to traditional business practices.

And don't feel that because you are majoring in one discipline, you can't participate in a club that corresponds to another discipline. Whether you are a marketing major or not, the Marketing Club will provide you with an opportunity to learn about marketing from business executives and through various professional activities. The Management Information Systems Club (MIS) will help you develop your skills and learn more about this dynamic field of study.

Business Honor Societies. Business colleges and disciplines also have honor societies. For example, *Beta Gamma Sigma* is the honorary society for colleges of business administration; *Beta Alpha Psi* is the national professional and honorary accounting fraternity; and the *Financial Management Association National Honor Society* recognizes outstanding achievement in the discipline of finance.

You cannot choose to join honor societies but instead you must be invited. This generally happens in your junior or senior year based on having achieved an academic record which places you in the top ten or twenty percent of the students in your major. I would encourage you to set a personal goal of membership in *Beta Gamma Sigma*. *Beta Gamma Sigma* is the business counterpart to *Phi Beta Kappa*, the honor society for liberal arts students. Membership in *Beta Gamma Sigma* is a very prestigious honor. This is an outstanding academic achievement that will impress future recruiters and employers.

Ethnic and Gender Based Student Organizations. Your university and your business college may have one or more ethnic-based student organizations. The most common of these organizations are the League of Black Business Students, Hispanic American Organization, Asian American Association and the International Student Organization to name just a few. The purpose of these organizations is to increase the academic and social growth of members of the respective ethnic group. However, membership is not restricted, and all who are committed to the purpose of the organization are welcome.

Business Student Council. All of the business student organizations may be organized into a business student council. The purpose of this *umbrella* organization is to coordinate activities sponsored jointly by several or all of the member organizations. Activities could include coordinating career fairs or inviting dignitaries to be speakers.

Benefits of Participation in Student Organizations.

When you join a student organization that is a chapter of a national society, paying your dues will make you a member of the national organization, and you will benefit from student activity programs conducted by the society. You will receive society publications and in some cases student magazines. You will be eligible to attend local, regional, and national meetings and conferences of the society. And you will be eligible to compete for individual awards, scholarships, fellowships, chapter awards and internships. But your greatest benefits will come from your participation in the chapter through its activities on your campus. Business student organizations provide benefits to their members in five major categories:

1)	Social interaction
2)	Personal development
3)	Professional development
4)	Academic development
5)	Service to the college and the community

The benefits that you will receive in each of these categories are discussed as follows.

Social Interaction.   Participation in business student organizations can help you develop relationships with students who have similar backgrounds, interests, and academic and career goals as you.   Close association with students in your academic major can enhance your academic success through the sharing of information and group study. Relationships you develop with fellow business students can continue long after your college days are over.

Student organizations can promote this social interaction through sponsorship of social functions such as mixers, parties, picnics, and athletic competitions.   Fund-raising activities such as car washes, raffles, jog-a-thons, and banquets can also promote social interaction among members.   A student lounge or study center can greatly enhance the social environment for student chapter members.

Personal Development.   Through participation in student organizations, you can develop leadership, organizational, and interpersonal skills so important to your success as a business professional.   As you will learn from your involvement in student organizations, it is a significant challenge to get a group of people to agree on a direction and to move efficiently in that direction.   Accomplishing this requires skills in communicating, persuading, listening, cooperating, delegating, reporting, managing, and scheduling.

A student organization can assist its members in developing their leadership and organizational skills by conducting leadership workshops and retreats and by sponsoring speakers on organizational management. The greatest lessons, however, result from opportunities to practice leadership skills.   The opportunities for this practice can be maximized by putting an organizational structure in place which provides leadership roles for as many people as possible. The ideal organization would involve an extensive committee structure organized around tasks to accomplish specific objectives (Membership Committee, Fund Raising Committee, Social Committee, Professional Development Committee).

__Professional Development__.   Participation in business student organizations can enhance your understanding of the business profession and the business work-world.   Much of the material to be presented in Chapter 5 can be "brought to life" through professional development activities conducted by student organizations.

Student organizations can sponsor speakers, videotape presentations, and field trips to local business and industry. They can organize career day programs in which business representatives meet with students to discuss employment opportunities. And they can sponsor seminars and workshops in important career development areas such as resume writing, interviewing skills, and job-search strategies.

__Academic Development__. Participation in business student organizations can enhance your academic performance through direct academic support activities.

Student organizations can sponsor mentor programs in which upper division (junior and senior) students assist lower division (freshman and sophomore) students.   Organizations can arrange for volunteer tutors, schedule review sessions and study groups. Some student organizations create their own study space, which can promote group study and sharing of information among their members.   Student organizations can also establish group challenge goals for average GPA and use peer pressure to keep members from "letting the organization down."

__Service to the College and the Community__. Participation in student organizations can provide you a vehicle for service to your college and the surrounding community.

Student organizations can sponsor visits to high schools to recruit students into the business programs, raise funds and use them to establish a scholarship, or carry out other service projects which benefit the business college.

Participation in Other Activities

In addition to participation in business student organizations, there are certain types of other activities that you might consider for your own personal development or for strengthening specific talents. Examples of these are writing for your campus newspaper, joining the debate club, or participating in musical or dramatic productions.

And don't forget student government—another excellent opportunity for personal growth and development. Eventually you may want to run for one of the many elected offices, but many positions are appointed. Go to the student government office and ask how you can become involved. **Who knows, maybe in a few years you'll be running for student body president!**

4.2 Participation in Extracurricular Projects

The quality of your education can be significantly enhanced through participation in extracurricular projects. Two types of such opportunities will be discussed here:

1) Student competitions

2) Undergraduate research

Student Competitions

In recent years, the number of student competitions available to business students has grown steadily. Some of these are paper studies only. Others involve papers combined with the design and presentation of a solution to an actual business situation. Some of the competitions are local university events. However, others involve competition against entries from other universities.

Major business corporations sponsor a number of the events. They are "judged" by business executives who are not only evaluating the solution, but future job applicants. Some of the competitions are open to individual students; but many involve competitions among teams of students.

Participation in case competitions will provide you with a significant, practical, "real-world" business experience. You will learn to work on a complex project, subject to strict deadlines, and requiring a high degree of cooperation and coordination. You will experience the negotiations, compromises, and difficult decisions that are characteristic of business projects. A significant investment of time will be required, but the rewards will be well worth the effort.

Your business college may be sponsoring or participating in one or more of these competitions on a regular basis. Check with your department chair. If you have an interest in an event that your college is not participating in, you may just be the catalyst to persuade them to do so.

The list below contains examples of various past student competitions from around the country. Many of the competitions require an invitation. Normally, a faculty sponsor from a college is required to make the "the first contact" on behalf of the individual or team. Your opportunity to participate in future competitions will be based on your willingness to work with your professor or department chair to seek out competitions which are appropriate to your course of study. [Please note: web addresses were current as of the time this text was printed. Updates are posted to the Discovery Press website at *www.discovery-press.com.*]

- **EDS Case Competition** - An MIS centered case study competition sponsored by Electronic Data Systems. For more information see their website:
  http://www.eds.com/about_eds/homepage/home_page_case_challeng e.shtml

- **College of Business Administration Loyola Marymount University Case Competition** - A business ethics case competition. Students are invited to research an ethical issue connected with an actual business. Sponsored by the Center for Business Ethics, College of Business Administration, Loyola Marymount University. For more information see their web site:
- *http://www.ethicsandbusiness.org/index2.htm* and select intercollegiate competition

- **University of Oregon New Venture Competition** – A young entrepreneurs competition. For more information see their website:
  http://darkwing.uoregon.edu/~uocomm/newsreleases/latest/mar98/P 032098_2.html

- **University of Lethbridge Case Competition** - Teams work together to analyze and make recommendations on a given management case. Cases can focus on any management specialty–from accounting to marketing to human resources. Sponsored by the University's Faculty of Management and KPMG Chartered Accountants. For more

information see their website:
http://www.linc.uleth.ca/notice/archive/12130.htm

- **The Marshall School International Invitational Case Competition** - An international university sponsored case competition for undergraduates. For more information see their website: *http://www.marshall.usc.edu/main/media/news/case.html*

- **Institute of Management Accounts Case Competition** – Each year the IMA sponsors a National Student Video Case Competition in which teams of students prepare a 15-minute videotaped solution to a case study. For more information see their website: *http://www.rutgers.edu/Accounting/raw/ima/students.htm* (and select student case competition) or *http://raw.rutgers.edu/raw/ima/students/casecomp.htm*

- **National Student Advertising Competition (NSAC)** - A student competition to create a comprehensive multimedia campaign that can be readily implemented by a real world client. For more information see their website: *http://www.aaf.org/nsac.html* and *http://www.aaf.org/collegechps.html*

- **SIFE (Students in Free Enterprise) Competitions** - Student-generated free market economic project competitions which are presented at regional and national competitions. For more information see their website: *http://www.sife.org/*

- **Anderson Tax Challenge** – A case competition for accounting students. For more information see their web site: *http://www.arthurandersen.com/Framesalt.asp?/taxchallenge/*

- **SCORE (Service Corps of Retorted Executives Association) Activities and Competitions** – A variety of competitions and activities are conducted by SCORE, a nonprofit association dedicated to entrepreneur education and the formation, growth and success of small business nationwide. Usually SCORE is affiliated with the local Chamber of Commerce. For information contact your local SCORE Chapter: *http://www.score.org/* and select "find score"

- **Small Business Development Centers Activities and Competitions -**
A variety of competitions sponsored by local Small Business
Development Centers (SBDC). For more information call your local
Chamber of Commerce and ask for the SBDC nearest you or see their
website:
http://www.smallbiz.suny.edu/roster.htm

Undergraduate Research

You can also broaden your education by working with business
professors on their research projects. Research projects generally involve
creating and organizing new knowledge and disseminating that knowledge
through publications in business journals and presentations at scholarly
meetings.

Your involvement with business faculty is primarily through their
teaching role. You may not realize that business professors are also
expected to conduct research. The amount of research expected of
professors varies from one university to the next.

External funding supports most research work. Faculty submit
proposals to outside agencies requesting funding to cover the costs of
conducting the research. One of the primary uses of the funding is to hire
student assistants. Although many of the students working on research
projects are graduate students pursuing either their M.B.A., M.S., or Ph.D.
degrees, opportunities also exist for undergraduate students to work on
research projects.

I would encourage you to seek out these opportunities to work on
research projects during your period of undergraduate study. Openings
may be listed at your university career planning and placement office, but
more likely you will have to speak to individual professors. You can get
information as to which professors have funded projects at the various
business department offices.

The benefits of an undergraduate research experience can be
significant. You will earn money to support the costs of your education.
You will also have the opportunity to work closely with a business
professor. Since other students will probably be working on the project,
you will learn how to work as a member of a team. An undergraduate
research experience will enable you to "try out" research to see if graduate
school is for you. Depending on the nature of the project, you will

develop your skills in specific areas such as computing or business analysis. It is possible that you will be listed as a co-author on papers resulting from the research and may even have the opportunity to present the results of your work at a student research conference.

4.3 Pre-Professional Employment

The *Employment Model* presented in Chapter 1 indicated five key factors that employers consider in selecting individuals for employment. One of these was business-related work experience.

A company considering you for employment when you graduate would like to see that you have had previous work experience. Work experience not only demonstrates interest, initiative, and commitment on your part, it also provides you with references—people you have worked for who can vouch for your abilities. Prospective employers also feel that the experience you have gained will reduce the time it takes for you to become productive in their environment.

Benefits of Pre-Professional Employment

Pre-professional employment can benefit you in many ways. Most obvious is that you will **earn money** to support the cost of your education. But the benefits are much more extensive than this. As previously mentioned, the experience you gain will **increase your marketability** when you seek permanent employment. Furthermore, the process of seeking pre-professional employment can be viewed as a dress rehearsal for the search you will eventually conduct for a permanent job. You will **develop important skills** related to preparing yourself for a job search, identifying potential employers, and presenting yourself to those employers.

Pre-professional employment will enhance your professional development as well. You will **gain exposure** to the business work world that will assist you in selecting your major course of study. You will gain a **better understanding** of the various business functions. You will have an opportunity to **apply your knowledge, skills, and abilities**. On your return to school, you will **better understand** how your academic coursework relates to the work-world. All of this should increase your motivation to succeed in business study.

Variety of Opportunities

Pre-professional employment can take the form of:

Internships

Summer jobs

Part-time jobs

Cooperative education ("co-op") experiences

Each of these types of pre-professional employment will be briefly discussed in the following sections.

Internships. Some institutions offer formal internship opportunities for students which are part of or replace academic classes for a semester or term. An internship is usually related to a specific project, and may or may not earn academic credit for the student. Student interns may or may not receive monetary compensation. Local businesses usually sponsor internships, in cooperation with the institution, to provide important "real world" experiences for students. The business benefits by getting help on problems that, while important, might not justify the hiring of a full-time professional employee.

Summer Jobs (Internships). Many business employers hire students during the summer. These summer jobs are often called internships. Many employers have a formal summer job (internship) program in which they bring in a specific number of students each summer.

The difference between a summer job and an internship is job content. If you decide to work on a road paving crew that would be a summer job. If decide to work in a business-related discipline and coordinate your activities with a faculty member that would an internship. Either way a summer job will provide you with many benefits; it will be a welcome break from the grind of the academic year; you will be able to make some extra money; and possibly you will earn some academic credit. Summer can be a time for rejuvenation. After a summer work experience, you are likely to return to school re-energized with renewed commitment.

I would suggest that you set a personal goal of working in a business discipline-related summer job (internship) for one or more of the summers during the period of your undergraduate study. One problem, however, is that student demand for summer jobs outpaces the supply. I would encourage you to adopt the positive, assertive attitude that if anyone is going to get a summer job, it's going to be you. Putting into practice the approaches for conducting a job search presented in subsequent sections of this chapter will give you a high probability of making that happen.

Part-time Jobs. You may also want to work on a part-time basis during the academic year. The availability of part-time jobs will depend on the location of your university. If your university is located in a major urban area, opportunities may be abundant. In contrast, if it is located in a small town, there may be few quality opportunities available within commuting distance.

Often students who do a good job during a summer work experience are invited to continue on a part-time basis during the academic year. Although the employer may benefit by having you continue to work, this may not be the best situation for you. It can be flattering to be invited to continue working during the academic year, and the money may be tempting. Make sure that you make a wise decision, which considers your overall academic and career goals.

There are some tradeoffs to consider when choosing between working in a non-professional job on campus and a discipline-related job off campus. The on-campus job will take less of your time since you will not have to commute. And it will probably be easier to fit in a few hours here and a few hours there. On the other hand, you will get more relevant experience from the discipline-related job and the pay will probably be better. However, it is likely to take more time and energy away from your studies.

If you do decide to work on campus, try to find a job that will complement your academic work. Working as a tutor, peer counselor, teaching assistant, grader, and undergraduate research assistant are examples of such positions.

One final thing to consider. Full-time business study is a full-time commitment. You can probably work up to twelve hours per week and take a full course load. If you work more than twelve hours per week, you should consider reducing your course load. Recall the guidelines presented in Chapter 2:

Hours worked	Max course load
12 hrs/wk	full load
20 hrs/wk	12 units
40 hrs/wk	8 units

Keep in mind that these are only guidelines. There are students who are able to work full-time and take a full load of courses. You will have to experiment with what works for you given your individual ability, background, energy level, and willingness to make personal sacrifices.

Cooperative Education. Your institution may offer Cooperative Education as an alternative learning experience. If you are interested, check with your academic advisor.

The U.S. Department of Education defines Cooperative Education programs as having alternating or parallel periods of academic study and employment related to the student's academic programs or professional goals. The work periods can range from part-time work while engaging in part-time study (parallel co-op) to the more traditional six-months-on, six-months-off (traditional co-op). The opportunity for parallel co-op is generally limited to universities located in areas having a significant number of nearby employers.

Cooperative education provides students with some distinct benefits. Among them are:

- Practical experience in business or industry

- Money to support college expenses

- A "foot in the door" in terms of seeking permanent employment upon graduation

Traditional co-op experiences will provide you with all the benefits described above, but because of the lengthier period of full-time employment, the experience gained is generally more meaningful than for summer jobs or part-time jobs. More significant assignments can be given as progressively more experience is gained over the six-month period. The benefits of co-op are even more pronounced when you participate in a second or third co-op experience at the same company.

The "down sides" of co-op are minimal. Participation in one or more traditional cooperative education work experiences will delay your graduation by up to one year. You may become "off sequence" with respect to your business courses. Check carefully with your academic advisor to ensure you select the appropriate schedule of courses. Also, some students have difficulty adjusting to their return to the university from a co-op experience. Six months of earning a good salary and having your nights and weekends free can become habit forming.

At most universities, participation in a co-op work experience is something the student may elect to do. Often, students receive academic credit for the co-op assignment, but this varies from institution to institution. The degree of assistance that universities provide to students seeking placement in co-op positions varies significantly. Universities that have a mandatory co-op program will generally have a well-staffed co-op office that identifies co-op positions and matches students with those positions. At the other extreme, students may be virtually on their own to find co-op positions with minimal or no help from the career planning and placement office.

How Do You Measure Up?

Regardless of the form of pre-professional employment opportunity you are seeking, your competitive position will be based primarily on three factors:

1) **Your level in the business curriculum**
2) **Your academic performance**
3) **Your personal qualifications**

As a freshman or sophomore you will have more difficulty finding employment because businesses generally prefer juniors and seniors— students closer to graduation. Junior and senior students bring a stronger educational background to their work. And the company values the opportunity to take a look at a student who will soon be a candidate for permanent employment.

But you can make up for your freshman or sophomore status by being strong in items #2 and #3. You could attend a summer school class and improve your GPA or take a free elective that will expand understanding of a specialized business concept. If you are a top student academically, businesses will be interested in developing an early relationship with you. The competition for top business students is keen. Businesses are well aware that hiring you after your freshman or sophomore year will give them the "inside track." The question they will ask themselves is "Are you worth the longer wait?"

Your personal qualifications will be a major factor in your success in landing a pre-professional employment position. The "bottom line" question that a prospective employer will ask is **"Will we enjoy having this student in our organization?"** The answer will result from an overall evaluation of your enthusiasm, initiative, communication skills, and ability to work with others. An employer will not be disappointed if you fail to solve their most pressing problem. But they will be very disappointed if you bring a negative, uncooperative, or unfriendly attitude to your work.

Regardless of how you measure up against the three factors discussed above, your chances of landing a quality business job while you are a student will depend to a great extent on how **you** go about your job search. Effort and approach were discussed in Chapter 1 as keys to your academic success. Similarly, they will be keys to your success in landing a summer job, part-time job, or co-op position. Conducting a job search not only takes considerable time and effort but will require that you put into practice effective strategies and approaches. Developing necessary job search skills will require significant preparation on your part.

A job search can logically be divided into the following steps:

1) Preparing yourself
2) Identifying opportunities
3) Applying for positions
4) Following up on interviews

Each of these steps will be discussed in the following sections.

What to Do BEFORE You Start a Job Search

Aside from getting the best grades you possibly can and developing yourself personally using the principles presented in Chapter 3, there are specific things you need to do to prepare yourself for a job search. You will need to develop a resume, learn how to write cover letters, and hone your interview skills.

Preparing a Resume. The resume is your main vehicle for presenting yourself to a potential employer. The key question to ask in preparing your resume is "If you were an employer, would you want to read this resume?" Employers generally prefer well-written, one-page chronological resumes. Visual impact and appearance are extremely important. Content should include:

Identifying data (name, address, and telephone number)

Employment objective

Educational background

Work experience

Specialized skills

Activities and affiliations

Honors and awards

Assistance in developing your resume should be available through your career planning and placement office. Most business schools offer a business communications course, which will include a lesson on resume development. Other excellent references are available to guide you in the development of your resume. [2,3]

Preparing a Cover Letter. Whether you are contacting prospective employers by mail or in person, you should always include a cover letter with your resume. And you should create a customized, individualized cover letter for each resume you send out. According to an article in the National Business Employment Weekly [4], if you want your cover letter "to score a direct hit in your quest for interviews:"

- Write to a specific person in the firm, using name and title. This should be the person who makes the hiring decision or for whom you'd work, if hired.

- In your opening paragraph, write something that demonstrates your knowledge of the organization and shows that it isn't a form letter.

- Communicate something about yourself that relates to the specific employer's needs and discusses the benefits you can contribute.

- Ask for a meeting (don't call it an interview). In your closing, be sure to state that you would like to meet and will call in a few days to schedule a time.

- Type your letter on one page, preferably on personalized stationery.

One additional hint: As you prepare your cover letter, pay careful attention to organization of ideas, grammar, and spelling. Many employers use the cover letter to evaluate a candidate's writing skills.

Developing Your Interviewing Skills. The final area in which you need to prepare yourself is in the area of interviewing skills. Think of an interview like the *final examination* in a course. You wouldn't consider taking a final exam without extensive preparation. If you want to verify for yourself that you are prepared to do well in an interview, seek out a friend or fellow student and get them to ask you the following questions:

What was your favorite course?
How would you describe yourself?
What are your long-range career goals?
How would you describe your ideal job?
Why should I hire you?
Explain your grade point average?
Have you taken on any leadership roles in student organizations?
Can you give any examples of where you worked effectively with a team of other students?
What are your greatest strengths?
What are your major shortcomings?
How would your skills meet our needs?

> **What have you accomplished that you are the most proud of?**

> **What would you like to know about us?**

I hope that the above exercise will convince you of the need to put significant effort into preparing yourself for interviews.

In addition to preparing to answer questions, there are other things you should do to prepare for an interview. Learn as much as you can about the company, the job you are seeking, and the person who will be interviewing you. Also develop a list of questions to ask the interviewer. Being inquisitive and asking good questions is a good way to impress.

Your campus career planning and placement office can also assist you in developing your interviewing skills. Not only does that office conduct workshops, but it can offer you a mock interview in which you are interviewed by a staff member assuming the role of a corporate recruiter, who then gives you valuable feedback. Another way for you to gain insight into how well you interview is to videotape yourself responding to interview questions. Videotaping is a powerful tool that you should try to utilize.

Finally, there are a number of excellent references at the end of this chapter that can assist you in developing your interviewing skills [5,6].

Identifying Employment Opportunities

There are many ways you can go about identifying employment opportunities. Your career planning and placement office is a good place to start. They arrange interviews, but most of these are for students seeking permanent employment. However, the list of companies that conduct on-campus interviews for business graduates is an excellent source of leads for you to pursue. If your placement office doesn't provide opportunities to interview for summer or part-time jobs, they may have a bulletin board on which they post such job listings. You can check with your department chair or a business faculty member. Finally, the campus alumni office and the alumni chapters around the country are also potential resources for identifying employment opportunities.

Attend any job fairs or career day programs held on your campus. Do not wait until your are senior. Freshman, sophomores and juniors can benefit significantly from these events. Try to establish personal relationships with the business representatives. Be friendly and sell yourself—maybe wrangle an invitation to visit their facility.

Networking is one of the best ways to find a job.

> ## View everyone you know or meet as a possible lead to a job!

Obvious candidates for networking include your professors, fellow students, business professionals who come to your campus to give a talk, and professionals you meet at meetings of business societies. But anyone from neighbors and relatives to your doctor or people you know through church or other community affiliations may be able to open a door for you. Remember that people enjoy helping others. If you ask people for advice, they will gladly offer it. One warning however: People do not like to be responsible for others. Don't make others feel that getting you a job is their responsibility.

Don't think of networking as a one-way street. Just as others can be a resource for you, you can be a resource for others. As you progress through the process of preparing yourself for your job search and carrying out that job search, you will gain valuable information that will be useful to others. Who knows? You may help a fellow student get a summer job this year, which will result in that student opening doors for you next year.

There are many other sources of information about business employers. The classified ads in the newspaper can give you a clue as to who is hiring, even though the positions advertised will not be for you. Your university reference librarian can assist you in finding publications that list employers. The *National Business Employment Weekly* published by the *Wall Street Journal* is good source, which should be available in your library. There are other publications [7,8], which contain good leads.

There are a number of job listings posted on electronic bulletin boards and accessible through the Internet system. Your career planning and placement office should be able to assist you in accessing these job listings. Many of the jobs may not be for your specific discipline, but the listings can guide you as to which companies are hiring.

Application Procedures

As implied in the previous section, in a short time you can identify more leads than you will ever have time to pursue. The purpose of this section is to provide you guidance as to how to apply for a pre-professional employment position.

The most straightforward way to apply for a position is to call a potential employer and find out the name and title of the individual in charge of their student-hiring program. Send this individual a cover letter and resume. The cover letter should indicate that you will follow-up with a telephone call within two weeks. The shortcoming of mailing your cover letter and resume is that your application may very well get into a large pile, which usually do not get serious consideration. The challenge for you is to find a way to get your application out of that pile.

Your primary goal is to get to an interview. An interview will give you the best opportunity to "sell" yourself using the interviewing skills you develop. But it is not so easy to get an interview. Industry representatives, whether they be in the human relations department or in the line organization, are generally very busy. They have too many candidates for employment and too little time.

If you do get an interview, you can follow the guidance presented in the earlier section on _Developing Your Interviewing Skills_. But you don't have to wait to be invited for an interview. You can take the initiative and arrange an "informational interview."

Informational Interviews. The informational interview is **_not_** a job interview. It is an information gathering session. In a job interview, the employer is interviewing you. In an informational interview, you are interviewing the employer.

How do you arrange an informational interview? A good way is through _networking_. Perhaps through a friend or a member of your family you get the name of a business executive at a local company. You then telephone that person, using the name of your friend or family member as a reference, and ask for 20 or 30 minutes of their time to learn about the kind of work that they do and about the company.

Although personal referrals are helpful, you can arrange informational interviews without them. Any alumnus of your business program would very likely be willing to meet with you. Or you can just use the fact that you are a business student and would like to learn more about career opportunities as entree. Call a local firm and ask to speak to the vice president in charge of the area most closely related to your discipline (e.g., vice president of marketing). If you can't reach her or him, you will probably be referred to someone at a lower level. You can then truthfully say that you were referred by the vice president's office and would like to meet with that person to learn more about what the company does that relates to your discipline.

In preparing for the informational interview, make up a list of questions you plan to ask. The following are some examples:

What do you do in your current position?
What are the most satisfying aspects of your work?
What is your educational background?
Which of the courses you took in college have been the most useful to you?
What was your first job after college?
How did you go about getting that position?
How is your company's business picture?
What is the future hiring situation?
Do you think that it is important for students to get business-related work experience?
Can you advise me as to how to go about getting a position that will give me that experience?

Remember that people enjoy helping others and giving advice. And people like to talk about themselves. Recall the story of the coal salesman, Mr. Knaphle, in Chapter 2. By showing that you are interested in other people and want to learn from them, they will become interested in you. You may find that they offer to help you get a summer job without you even asking. If not, you can always send them an application for employment at a future date.

Post-Interview Actions

Whether a job interview or an informational interview, it is important that you follow up. Always send a thank-you letter. Few people do, so it will help you be remembered positively. Thank the interviewer for his or her time and interest. Be sure to mention some specific information you learned from them which you found particularly useful. If you are following up on a job interview, express genuine interest in the job opportunity. In your letter, leave the door open for you to contact them in the future.

4.4 Education is a Two-way Street

I'm sure you have heard someone say "I'm not going to vote. My vote doesn't really count." In one way, that view makes sense. After all, with millions of votes cast, one vote isn't really likely to make a difference. But what if everyone adopted the view that their vote isn't important? Since we can't afford to have everyone decide not to vote, it's not right for one to do so.

How do you view your relationship with your university or college? Do you feel that you have something to offer your institution? Or do you feel that your contributions are not important—that what one student does cannot really make a difference? I hope you see the parallel with the importance of voting and realize that it is important that you "cast your vote" with your university—that you put something back into the institution that is giving you so much.

President John F. Kennedy motivated an entire generation of young Americans when he said:

> *Ask not what your country can do for you,*
> *ask what you can do for your country.*

I would urge you to ask, "What can I do for my institution?" Doing things that will benefit your institution is a real "win-win." The institution wins because the things you do will make it a better place for its students, faculty, and staff. You win not only because you will reap direct rewards from experiences gained through what you do, but also because the quality of your institution will be improved.

And putting something into your institution can continue throughout your lifetime. After you graduate, you will be an alumnus of the university. As an alumnus, you will have the ongoing opportunity to enhance your institution through both contributions of your time and money. The value of your education is related to the image others have of your university or college. If the image of your university improves, even after you have graduated, the value of your education will be enhanced.

The purpose of this section is to discuss some of the ways in which you can put something back into your university or college while you are an undergraduate student. Doing many of the things we have already discussed such as performing well in your classes and becoming actively involved in extra-curricular activities will by their very nature benefit your university. I'm sure you can think of many other ways you can serve your university. We will discuss three of these briefly:

1) Providing feedback

2) Serving as an ambassador

3) Helping other students

Feedback is the Lifeline of Any Organization

You are your institution's primary customer. You know best what you need and whether you are getting it. You should make every effort to let those in decision-making positions know how the institution is serving its customers. And don't feel that you can only give feedback about things you don't like. Positive feedback can have as much or more value in bringing about positive change than negative feedback.

You will be given some formal opportunities to provide feedback. Perhaps the best example of this is when you are invited to complete student opinion surveys about your professors' classroom performance. Please take these surveys seriously. They not only give feedback to your professors which they can use for self-improvement, the results of the student opinion surveys are used as part of the basis for decisions on tenure, promotion, and merit salary increases. Generally, the surveys consist of a series of numerical questions followed by the opportunity to write narrative comments. I would strongly encourage you to write detailed comments. As a professor, I found the comments much more useful than the numerical results.

You will undoubtedly have other opportunities to make formal input. You may be invited to write letters of support for professors; you may receive surveys designed to measure the overall campus climate; or you may see a notice inviting students to meet with the dean or department chair to give feedback. I hope you take full advantage of these and other invitations to give feedback.

You can also give unsolicited input. Be liberal with positive feedback. As we discussed in Chapter 2, let your professors know when you like the subject or like their teaching. Tell the dean or department chairs about anything you like. People are less receptive to negative feedback, so you should be more selective with negative criticism. Constructive criticism is by far the better approach. If you really feel that something important is not right, don't hesitate to make an appointment to see the dean or the department chair and tell him or her about it. But if you do, make every effort to present yourself in a tactful, respectful, and rational manner.

I strongly recommend whenever you submit a criticism that you also submit two or three suggestions that would correct the situation. Making positive suggestions is the essence of "constructive criticism." Your suggestions may or may not be used but you will accomplish two important objectives:

1. You will be identified as positive agent for change and not as a "whiner".

2. The next time you want to submit a criticism the "door" will be easier to open.

Continuing the application of this process will serve you well not only during your academic career, but also throughout your professional career.

A Personal Story

Once I was a member of the planning team working on a critical organization-wide auditing project for the regional manager of a national organization. Our team identified a potential problem with the implementation plan. We all agreed that we should meet with the regional manager to brief him on the problem. As the briefing concluded the regional manger asked us what course or courses of action we were recommending as a solution. Our team leader stated we were looking for his guidance. The regional manager sat back in his chair, clasped his hands and in a very even voice stated "If I knew all the answers, I would not need all of you. I hired you to identify problems and

> *recommend solutions. Anyone can bring me problems." From that day forward, I have always provided at least one course of corrective action for every problem I identify.*

Serving as an Ambassador

You are also your university's best ambassador. There are both formal and informal opportunities for you to serve in ambassador roles. Your university may have a formal *ambassador organization* of students who represent the university at a variety of events. Ambassadors conduct special tours; host receptions, dinners, or special events; serve as ushers; and greet distinguished visitors and alumni.

Your university may also have a community service organization similar to the Educational Participation in Communities (EPIC) program. This type of organization provides you with the opportunity to volunteer for community service assignments in schools, hospitals, community centers, and other human service agencies.

You can also create your own ambassador activities. Return to your high school or other high schools and speak to teachers and students there on behalf of the university. In fact, "word of mouth" is one of the university's best image builders. When you speak to anyone off-campus, take the view that you are representing the university. Put forth the most positive perspective you can. Keep your complaints on-campus and make them to someone who can do something about them.

Helping Other Students

Can you recall times when others students helped you? What did they do for you? Perhaps they pointed you toward a great teacher; or provided you with information about some regulation or campus resource that really benefited you; or gave you some free tutoring which clarified a point you were stuck on.

Don't always be the one who is seeking help from others. Look for opportunities to help other students. Although what you have to offer will increase as you progress through the curriculum, even as a freshman you can help other students. This help can be either informal through contact you initiate or through work as a volunteer in more structured situations. Volunteer to serve as a computer consultant in the business computer lab. Volunteer to work as a peer tutor in your university learning resource center. Or volunteer to work as a peer adviser with a special program for "at risk" students.

You will find that when you help others, you will get more out of it than they do. You will develop your interpersonal communication skills, increase your knowledge, and feel good about yourself for having done it.

Summary

The purpose of this chapter was to introduce you to a number of activities you can engage in, in addition to your formal academic work, which will broaden and enhance the quality of your education. Each of the suggested activities will build your interpersonal communication, teamwork, organizational, and leadership skills, which are critically important to your success.

We described opportunities for participation in student organizations, particularly those organizations based in the business college. This participation can aid you in building relationships with other business students, in your personal and professional development, and in your academic achievement. Furthermore, student organizations can provide a vehicle for service to the business college and the community.

Next, we discussed the value of participation in extracurricular projects including student competitions and research projects. These activities can take a considerable time commitment on your part, but the return can be enormous.

The importance of gaining discipline-related work experience through pre-professional employment including summer jobs, part-time jobs, cooperative education experiences ("co-op"), and internships was discussed. We also presented approaches and strategies you should use in seeking employment. Working on developing your skills in this area over the period of your undergraduate study will be invaluable to you when you seek employment as you approach graduation.

Finally, we described several ways you can give something back to your university. As its customer, you can provide valuable feedback. As its best ambassador, you can represent it with external constituencies. And you can be of great help to other students, just as other students have been and will continue to be of help to you.

Most of the activities suggested in this chapter will require a certain amount of initiative on your part. They are not mandatory. Unlike your formal academic work, no one will require you to participate and no one will check up on whether you do it. But the return on investment can be even greater than the return that you receive from your formal coursework. The activities outlined in this chapter truly represent your opportunity to take responsibility for the *quality* of your education.

REFERENCES

1. U.S. Department of Education, *Cooperative Education*, Biennial Evaluation Report FY93-94, (*www.ed.gov/pubs/Biennial/524.html*), 1998.

2. Jackson, Tom and Jackson, Ellen, *The New Perfect Resume*, Main Street Books, 1996.

3. Yate, Martin John, *Resumes that Knock 'Em Dead*, 3rd Edition, Bob Adams, Inc., 260 Center Street, Holbrook, Massachusetts, 1997.

4. Jackson, Tom, "Resumes, Cover Letters and Interviews," *National Business Employment Weekly*, October 11-17, 1991.

5. Medley, H. Anthony, *Sweaty Palms, The Neglected Art of Being Interviewed*, Ten Speed Press, P.O. Box 7123, Berkeley, California, 1992.

6. Yate, Martin John, *Knock 'Em Dead with Great Answers to Tough Interview Questions*, Published by Bob Adams, Inc., 260 Center Street, Holbrook, Massachusetts, 1990.

7. *The Hidden Job Market 1997: A Job Seeker's Guide to America's 2,000 Little-Known, Fastest-Growing High-Tech Companies*, Peterson's Guides, Princeton, New Jersey, 1997.

8. *Graber, Steven et al. (Eds.), The National JobBank 1998*, Bob Adams, Inc., 260 Center Street, Holbrook, Massachusetts, 1997. (Note: There are 20 JobBank books, each covering a key U.S. job market)

Exercises

1. Develop a list of all business student organizations which operate in the business college at your university.

2. Are you an active member of one or more of the organizations you listed under Problem 1? If not, join the one you are the most interested in.

3. Once you have joined ask for information on all scholarships, fellowships, and awards to students by the organization. Share this information with fellow students. See if you are eligible for one of them and if so apply.

4. Find out if the student chapter you joined is organized to accomplish the five purposes outlined in Section 4.1. If not, suggest that a committee structure be put in place to accomplish each of these purposes (e.g., Social Committee, Professional Development Committee, Personal Development Committee, Academic Development Committee, Service Committee). Volunteer to chair one of these committees and develop a plan for the next year's activities.

5. Visit the office of your university-wide student government. Arrange to meet the student body president and ask him or her whether there are any open committee assignments you could volunteer for.

6. Find out whether your business college has participated in any of the student competitions listed in Section 4.2. If there is one or more, which one(s)? Consider getting involved in the competition.

7. If the answer to Problem 6 is "none," pick the one you are most interested in. Contact the sponsor of the competition to obtain detailed information on the event. Try to persuade your college to participate.

8. Find out how many full-time faculty there are in your college of business. Determine how many of them have one or more funded research projects. Find out how many of them employ undergraduate students to work on their research projects. Make a commitment to seek such an opportunity during your period of undergraduate study.

9. Determine whether your college has a formal cooperative education program in which it assists students with placement in co-op assignments (Note: The co-op program may be operated university-wide rather than by each academic unit). If there is a formal co-op program, visit the co-op office and find out how you can go about applying for a co-op position.

10. Visit your career planning and placement office. Ask if you can get a list of all companies that interview on campus for business graduates.

Pick one of the companies and research it. Determine when representatives from that company will visit campus next and plan to be there.

11. Do a personal assessment based on the three factors listed in the section on "How Do You Measure Up?" which indicate how well you will compete for pre-professional employment positions. If you are not satisfied with the outcome, what can you do to improve it?

12. Using the ideas presented in the section on "Preparing a Resume," develop your resume. Ask several people to critique it. These people could be fellow students, professors, placement office staff, or business professionals. Revise your resume based on the input you get. Commit to having a resume that is "ready to go" throughout your college years.

13. Write a cover letter seeking a summer job with the company you selected in Problem 10. Have the cover letter critiqued by several people and revise it until you are satisfied with it. Send the letter and your resume to the company early in the spring term.

14. Get a friend or fellow student to ask you the questions presented in the section on "Developing Your Interviewing Skills." Have the person critique your answers.

15. Prepare a written response to each of the questions presented in the section on "Developing Your Interviewing Skills." Practice your answers and then repeat Problem 14. Did you note any difference?

16. Make up ten additional questions that you think you might be asked in an interview for a summer job. Prepare responses to those questions.

17. Make a list of ten companies you would like to work for in the summer using the methods outlined in the section on "Identifying Employment Opportunities." Plan a campaign to apply for a pre-professional employment position with each of them.

18. Evaluate the list of questions presented in the section on *Informational Interviews*. Rate each question on a scale of 0 to 10. Think up five additional questions that you would like to ask. Rate those questions. Take the total list of fifteen questions and select ten you would feel comfortable asking a business professional. Order the questions in what you feel is the most logical order.

19. Pick three of the companies from the list of ten in Problem 17. Either through networking or through a telephone call identify a person from each company with whom you can conduct an *Informational Interview*. Arrange these interviews. Write a critique discussing how each interview went. Don't forget to send a follow-up letter after each interview.

20. Make up a list of questions you would ask a professor during an Informational Interview. Pick one of your business professors and seek a 20 to 30 minute meeting with him or her. Write a critique of the Informational Interview.

21. Write down ten things that you think are positive about your university. Rank them in order of importance. Pick ten different people (students, faculty members, department chair, dean). Tell each one of the people you picked about one of the items on your list. How did they respond?

22. Find out whether your college or the university has any service-oriented clubs. Write a one-page description of what one of the service organizations does. Would you be interested in joining the service club?

Chapter 5
BUSINESS AS A PROFESSION

Introduction

The purpose of this chapter is to introduce you to the world of business. First we will define the statement **"business as a profession."**

Next we will discuss the **rewards and opportunities** that can come to you when you are successful in graduating with your degree in business. Having a clear picture of the payoff will be a key factor in motivating you to make the personal sacrifice and put in the hard work required to succeed in such a challenging and demanding field of study.

Next, we'll discuss the various **business disciplines**, the **job functions** of business professionals, and the **major career opportunities** available to business graduates.

Finally, we will open your **horizons to the future** by describing those fields that show the greatest promise for growth.

5.1 Business as a Profession

Why did you choose business as your major? Perhaps because you were good in math, one of your teachers or counselors recommended that you study business. Or maybe you are doing it to please your parents, or you were told it would be a sure way to get a job, or because you don't know what else to do. It is very likely that you don't know a great deal about business as a profession. Few students do.

You Tend to Be More Aware of Other Fields

As you have grown up, you have been exposed to teachers, doctors and dentists, engineers, ministers and rabbis, and pharmacists. You have seen lawyers at work on TV shows such as *The Practice*. Through your coursework you have developed some understanding of what mathematicians and scientists do. However, it is doubtful that you have had much exposure to the world of business, at least to this point. The exposure you have had has probably been indirect, through contact with the products and services that business provides.

How important is it to you to graduate in business? How strong are your motivation and your commitment? Regardless of your reasons for being here, it is critically important that you develop a strong motivation. In Chapter 1, **determination to persist** was identified as a key factor for success in business study. Business is a demanding field of study. Even a student with excellent preparation and strong ability will not succeed without a high level of commitment.

An important aspect of developing your commitment to business study is increasing your awareness of business as a profession and of the opportunities and rewards that you will receive when you graduate. After all, how can you expect to make the personal sacrifices and put in the hard work required unless you have a clear picture of what the "return" is and how that return will enhance your life?

A Working Definition of Business

Students often come to my office and state confidently "I want to study business." I make it a point to ask them "What area of business do you want to study and why?" Most students have difficulty responding. I am not surprised. _Business_ is such a varied field that offers a broad variety of options and opportunities. Because of this, no simple definition is adequate. However, the _American Heritage Dictionary_ provides a good working definition [1]:

> _**Business**_ _is the occupation or work, or trade in which a person is engaged; Commercial, industrial, or professional dealings; The buying and selling of commodities or services; Any commercial establishment, such as a store_.

Possibly Calvin Coolidge, our 30th president gave the best and most appropriate definition, when he said,

"The business of America is Business."

Learning about Business is a Lifelong Process

Learning about business will be a lifelong process, but it should begin now. Take advantage of every opportunity that presents itself. Start by studying this chapter thoroughly.   Attend seminars on career opportunities, go on field trips to industry, and talk to business professionals at career day programs. Browse the resource library in your career planning and placement office. Become active in the student organizations corresponding to your major and to other business majors. Learn from your professors. Read biographies of successful business people [2,3,4]. You can learn a great deal from such role models. If you have a summer job in a company, be curious and inquisitive. Look around and talk to managers of different departments and find out what they do.

Over time, these efforts will pay off and your understanding of business will increase. Increased knowledge will bring increased motivation.

5.2 Rewards and Opportunities of a Career in Business

Business offers a wealth of opportunities. You can choose from many different professions: banking, manufacturing, construction, food industry, retail industry, etc. You can choose a job that is unique and highly selective, such as an insurance actuary, or you can choose a wide-open field such as a human resource generalist. Business students are represented in large numbers as shown by the data below for 1994/95 college graduates.

Bachelor's Degrees Conferred - 1994/95
Reference: U.S. Department of Education 1997[5]

Major	Number of 1994/95 College Graduates	Percent of Total
Business	**234,323**	**20 %**
Social Science and History	128,154	11 %
Mathematics	13,723	1 %
Education	106,079	9 %
Biological and Life Sciences/	55,984	5 %
Health Professions	79,855	7 %
Psychology	72,083	6 %
Engineering	62,342	5 %
All Other Majors	407,591	36 %
TOTAL	1,160,134	100.0%

So why choose to study business? Why seek to become one of the twenty percent of college graduates who receive a degree in business? What are the benefits that will come to you when you graduate in business?

The rewards and opportunities of a career in business are numerous. I have been involved in many discussions with students, parents, counselors, and faculty for the expressed purpose of identifying the benefits and rewards. Small groups would identify just a few while large groups would generally develop a list of thirty to forty items. Some are more important than others, depending on personal preferences. To one person, being well paid may be #1. Someone else may be attracted by the opportunity to do challenging work. Still another person may value business as a career because it will enable them to make a difference in people's lives.

With reference to Dave Letterman, my "Top Ten List'" for choosing business in rank order is:

Top Ten List

1. **Job satisfaction**
2. **Opportunity to make a difference in society**
3. **Intellectual development**
4. **Challenging work**
5. **Opportunity to understand how the world works**
6. **Variety of career opportunities**
7. **Avenues for expressing your own creativity**
8. **Financial security**
9. **Prestige**
10. **Professional work environment**

1. Job Satisfaction

What do you think is the #1 cause of unhappiness among people in the United States. Health problems? Family problems? Financial problems? No. Studies have shown that, by far, the number-one cause of unhappiness among people in the U.S. is **job dissatisfaction**.

Do you know people who dislike their job? People who get up every morning and wish they didn't have to go to work? People who watch the clock all day and can't wait until their workday is over? People who work only to earn an income so they can enjoy the time that they don't have to work? Maybe you have been in that situation. Lots of people are.

Throughout my career, it has been very important to me that I enjoy my work. After all, I will spend eight plus hours a day, five days a week, fifty weeks a year, for over forty years working. This represents almost half of my waking time. Which would you rather be, a person who spends half of their life working and dislikes every minute of it, or a person who spends half of their life working and loves it? I hope you agree with me that it is extremely important to find a life's work that is satisfying, work that you enjoy.

Business could very well be that life's work. It certainly has been for me and for many of my colleagues over the years. There are numerous reasons why work can be satisfying. Some of these are discussed in the following sections.

2. Opportunity to Make a Difference in Society

I hope that you are motivated by a need to do something worthwhile in your career, something that will make a difference in society. Business can certainly be that career.

Just about everything that business professionals do can benefit society. The business of the transportation systems helps people and products move about so easily. Construction companies build the buildings where we live and work. Manufacturing companies produce the products we use such as cars, home appliances, sporting goods, computers, TVs, and medical equipment. Some form of business impacts every aspect of our lives.

Depending on your value system, you may not view all business as a positive difference or benefit to society. For example, business provides military equipment like missiles, tanks, bombs, artillery, and fighter airplanes. Business also provides us with pesticides, cigarettes, liquor, fluorocarbons, and asbestos. You will, of course, need to decide which career you will pursue. Keep in mind the most effective way to bring about a positive change in a business activity is to work in the business and effect changes rather than complain about the business from the outside.

You will have the opportunity to work on projects that are beneficial to society such as creating jobs in underdeveloped countries, establishing ethical and environmentally friendly business practices, and developing financial investment products which lead to retirement security. Maybe you will use your business degree to enter the political world and provide us with the leadership to finally achieve world peace.

3. Intellectual Development

Business education will "exercise" your brain. Through this exercise, mental abilities including your ability to think logically and to solve problems, and communicate more effectively will develop. This is not unlike developing your muscles by working out in a gym. Research is teaching us more about the potential for developing our minds. For example, we know that the brain is made up of as many as 180 billion neuron cells. Each neuron cell has a large number of tentacle-like protrusions called dendrites. The dendrites make it possible for each neuron cell to receive signals (synapses) from thousands of neighboring neuron cells. These "neural networks" are determined in large part by our experience. When we study and learn, we develop new connections in our brain.

One of the things I value most about my business education is that it developed my logical thinking ability. I have a great deal of confidence in my ability to deal effectively with problems. And this is not limited to "business" problems. I feel that I can use the problem solving skills and approaches I learned through my business education to take on the tasks of becoming a homeowners association president, dealing with a car salesman, buying a house, planning for retirement, planning a vacation, seeking a job, organizing a wedding, raising money for a homeless shelter, or writing this book. I'm sure that you will also come to value the role your business education will play in developing your mind and your ability to solve problems and complete tasks.

4. Challenging Work

Do you like intellectual stimulation? Do you enjoy taking on challenging problems? Not everyone does. Some people like to do things that are easy. If you like challenges, business could be for you. Certainly, while you are in college you will face many challenging assignments. But, as the saying goes, "you ain't seen nothing yet." In the work-world, there is no shortage of challenging "opportunities." Any business professional will tell you that they face any number of problems every day. The problems or "opportunities" are what make the job interesting and worthwhile. After all if there were no problems or opportunities, what would be the need for the position.

In the past, "real-world" business problems were quite different from most of the problems you would see in your college classrooms. New teaching paradigms, computers, and more efficient communications processes have lead to whole new approaches to "classroom problems". Although not exactly the same as the real world where virtually all problems are open-ended, the classroom environment is changing. There may no longer be a single answer printed in the back of the book. The professor may no longer inform you if you are right or wrong, but evaluate your application of business theories and your thought processes. You will generally be required to select the best solution from among many possible solutions, and defend that position with business logic. Each solution will have its own set of rewards and costs. It will be up to you to persuade others that your solution provides the best return on investment.

5. Opportunity to Understand How the World Works

Do you know what a mutual fund is? Do you understand the difference between common stock and preferred stock? Do you know what a JIT inventory system is and why it can potentially provide the company you work for with a substantial savings over traditional inventory methods? Do you understand corporate tax rates? Did you know that it is possible to buy a company that is losing money and then sell off the "parts" for a substantial profit? Do you know what you can and cannot do with respect to the hiring and firing of employees? Your business education will help you to understand and deal with each of the above questions and many more just like them.

Furthermore, there are many issues facing our society that depend on business to provide solutions. When will automobile manufacturers provide us with an economically feasible mass produced environmentally clean vehicle? Fossil fuels will not last forever. When will a safe, renewable and economic source of energy be developed? What about our transportation infrastructure? Do we need faster trains, automated roads, more supersonic aircraft? Why can the Japanese build better quality automobiles? Can we better manage our agricultural industry and eliminate world hunger? What can be done to provide a job and a decent standard of living for all citizens of our country?

Your business education will equip you to understand the world around you and to develop informed views regarding important social, political, and economic issues facing our nation and the world. Who knows, maybe this understanding will lead you into politics.

6. Variety of Career Opportunities

Would you like to work in a bank? Create the next round of Super Bowl advertisements for your company? How about developing the computer program to solve the "Year 2000" problem for your organization? Business people can and do solve these kinds of problems but there is so much more. The day you walk down the aisle to receive your degree in business, a tremendous range of opportunities will be open to you. In fact, there is virtually nothing you cannot do from that day forward. You can become a politician, professor, manager, doctor, or lawyer.

A Personal Story

> *When I was a freshman no one told me of the variety of career opportunities I could pursue as business graduate. My first job after graduation was in the air traffic control field and budget management. I later became an instructor in electronics and operational management techniques. I eventually joined the College of Business Administration at Notre Dame where I have been able to pursue my interest in teaching and academic administration. I often think back to that first day in college. I remember how apprehensive I felt. Is this the right field of study for me? What kind of job will I be qualified for? My business education prepared me for a lifetime of opportunities and I am not finished yet!*

Here are a few more opportunities you may not have considered:

- If you are imaginative and creative, become an entrepreneur and start your own business.

- If you want to help the less fortunate, you might consider running a homeless shelter or working for a major charity.

- If you like to organize and expedite projects, look into production management.

- If you are persuasive and like working with people, look into becoming a management consultant or even a federal arbitrator.

7. Expressing Your Creativity

Business, by its very nature, is a creative field. Business professionals are involved in developing solutions to open-ended, real-world problems to which there is generally no single, correct answer but many possible solutions. Ultimately, the job is to choose the best solution from among those that have been identified. However, the actual "best" solution may have been overlooked. The opportunity for creative thinking in solving business problems is unlimited. Unfortunately, we are often unable to overcome certain barriers to creative thinking, such as tradition, false assumptions, negative thinking, habits, fear of failure, and discomfort with ambiguity.

An excellent book that could help you improve your creativity is *Creative Problem Solving: Thinking Skills for a Changing World* by Edward and Monika Lumsdaine [6]. According to the Lumsdaines:

> **CREATIVITY** is playing with imagination and possibilities, leading to new and meaningful connections and outcomes while interacting with ideas, people, and the environment.

This could almost be the definition of what business professionals do. And the need for business professionals to think creatively is greater now than ever before because we are in a time when the rate of social and technological changes has greatly accelerated. Only through creativity can we cope with and adapt to these changes. If you like to question, explore, discover, and create, then the business world could be the ideal place for you.

8. Financial Security

When I ask a class of business students to talk about their plans after college almost all students immediately say "make money." I am not surprised since most students do not have any money while in college.

But as you have seen in my "Top Ten List," I have ranked financial security as #8. Its not that business people don't make good money. They do! It's just that money is not my primary motivator and should not be your primary motivator.

I've always held the view that if you choose something that you like doing, work hard at it, and do it well, the money will take care of itself. I admit this is easy to say for someone who has a good job. However, I hope that you don't make money your primary reason to study business. Other things like job satisfaction, challenging work, intellectual development, and opportunities to benefit society will be much more important to the quality of your life and to your personal happiness.

If you do choose business, however, **you can be rewarded financially**. Successful business people are well paid. In fact, even business graduates with relatively little experience receive good starting salaries, as shown by the data below for 1995/96-college graduate's [7].

Beginning Offers to 1995/96 College Graduates

Discipline	Avg. Salary
Business	$28,942
Sciences	27,737
Agriculture & Natural Resources	24,496
Humanities & Social Sciences	23,802
Communications	23,063
Education	23,005

You may also be interested to know that of the 21,280 offers reported in this study, 8,342 (39 percent) went to business graduates—a discipline that make up only 21 percent of college graduates—twice on average as many offers as received by graduates in other disciplines.

9. *Prestige*

What is prestige? *Prestige* is defined as "the power to command admiration or esteem." You may have already experienced the prestige associated with being a business major. Perhaps you have stopped on campus to talk with another student and he or she asked you, "What's your major?" What reaction did you get when you said, "Finance"? Probably one of respect, something like "Good choice!" or "Your lucky. You won't have to worry about getting a job." And perhaps you asked the other student, "What's your major?" only to wish you hadn't asked after getting an apologetic response like, "I'm still an undecided major."

Business is a respected field of study, but sometimes a student is asked to rank professions that are more prestigious than business. "Medicine" usually comes up immediately. Doctors are well paid and highly respected for the essential role they play in helping people. I certainly want to have highly capable and well-trained people as my doctors. However, this does not mean that business is less prestigious. After all the medical profession is also a "business" and even doctors must understand the principles of business if they plan to continue their practice.

Generally after medicine, law or engineering will be mentioned. I'll argue against these and any others as being more prestigious than business. Whether you think they are or not, the point is that business is a highly respected profession. There is general agreement that business plays a primary role in sustaining our nation's international competitiveness, in maintaining our standard of living, in ensuring a strong national security, and in protecting public safety.

Business is essential to our:

International competitiveness
Standard of living
National security
Public safety

10. Professional Work Environment

In your business career, you will work in a professional environment. You will be treated with respect. You will work with other professionals. You will have a certain amount of freedom in choosing your work. And you will be in a position to influence the directions taken by your organization.

You will be provided with adequate workspace and the tools you need to do your work, including the latest computer equipment and software. You will also be provided with the secretarial and technical support staff you need to get your work done. After all, your employer will benefit from making sure you have what you need to do a good job.

You will not be required to punch a time clock. Rather, you will be judged on your productivity, i.e., on the quality and quantity of your work. You can usually expect to receive an annual merit salary increase, which will be based on your management's evaluation of your performance.

You will have the opportunity to learn and grow through both on-the-job training and formal training. Early on, your immediate supervisor will closely mentor you and bring you along through the assignment of progressively more challenging tasks. You will also learn from more experienced managers in your organization. And you will be offered seminars and short courses to enhance your knowledge. These may be conducted by the company or by an outside organization. Many employers will have an educational reimbursement program, which will pay for you to attend a local university to pursue a graduate degree or just to take courses for professional development.

As a professional, you will receive liberal benefits, which will typically include a retirement plan, life insurance, health insurance, sick leave, paid vacation, holidays, and savings or profit-sharing plans.

5.3 Business Disciplines and Associated Career Opportunties

Business students are generally classified by their fundamental academic discipline.

Accounting

Economics

Finance

Management (Organizational Behavior)

Management Information Systems

Marketing

These are the six largest so-called *traditional* areas of business (Note: Management Information Systems can be considered as part of Management or as a separate academic discipline). This list is not all-inclusive and there may be other fields of study in business at your institution.

The following sections present one example of a career opportunity under each of these traditional majors as identified by the Bureau of Labor Statistics [8]. You, of course, would not be limited to that career opportunity. In fact, these are just a few examples of your future opportunities. As a business graduate, the door will be wide open to you!

I would like to thank the Bureau of Labor Statistics for authorizing the use of this material. I would recommend you visit the Bureau's web site (*http://stats.bls.gov/oco/oco1000.htm*) for recent updates and additional information on business career opportunities.

The information associated with the career opportunities presented in the following sections has been organized into a consistent format to assist you in comparing opportunities from one field to the next. Each career area contains the following information:

Nature of the work
Working conditions
Employment
Training, other qualifications, and advancement
Job outlook
Earnings
Related occupations
Sources of additional information

5.4 Accountants and Auditors

Nature of the Work

Accountants and auditors prepare, analyze, and verify financial reports and taxes, and monitor information systems that furnish this information to managers in business, industry, and government. The major fields of accounting are public, management, and government accounting, and internal auditing.

Public accountants have their own businesses or work for public accounting firms. They perform a broad range of accounting, auditing, tax, and consulting activities for their clients, who may be corporations, governments, nonprofit organizations, or individuals.

Management accountants—also called industrial, corporate, or private accountants—record and analyze the financial information of the companies for which they work. Other responsibilities include budgeting, performance evaluation, cost management, and asset management. They are usually part of executive teams involved in strategic planning or new product development.

Internal auditors verify the accuracy of their organization's records and check for mismanagement, waste, or fraud.

Government accountants and auditors maintain and examine the records of government agencies, and audit private businesses and individuals whose activities are subject to government regulations or taxation.

Within each field, accountants often concentrate on one aspect of accounting. For example, many public accountants concentrate on tax matters, such as preparing individual income tax returns and advising companies of the tax advantages and disadvantages of certain business decisions. Others concentrate on consulting and offer advice on matters such as compensation or employee health care benefits; the design of accounting and data processing systems; and controls to safeguard assets. Some specialize in forensic accounting—investigating and interpreting bankruptcies and other complex financial transactions. Still others work primarily in auditing—examining a client's financial statements and reporting to investors and authorities that they have been prepared and reported correctly. However, accounting firms are performing less auditing relative to consulting services, which are more profitable.

Working Conditions

Accountants and auditors work in a normal office setting. Self-employed accountants may be able to do part of their work at home. Accountants and auditors employed by public accounting firms and government agencies may travel frequently to perform audits at clients' places of business, branches of their firm, or government facilities.

Most accountants and auditors generally work a standard 40-hour week, but many work longer, particularly if they are self-employed and free to take on the work of as many clients as they choose. Tax specialists often work long hours during the tax season.

Employment

Accountants and auditors held over one million jobs in 1996. They worked throughout private industry and government, but about one-third worked on salary for accounting, auditing, and bookkeeping firms, or were self-employed.

Many accountants and auditors were unlicensed management accountants, internal auditors, or government accountants and auditors. However, many are State-licensed Certified Public Accountants (CPA's), Public Accountants (PA's), Registered Public Accountants (RPA's), and Accounting Practitioners (AP's).

Most accountants and auditors work in urban areas, in which public accounting firms and central or regional offices of businesses are concentrated.

Many individuals with backgrounds in accounting and auditing are full-time college and university faculty; others teach part time while working as self-employed accountants, or as salaried accountants for private industry or government.

Training, Other Qualifications, and Advancement

Most accountant and internal auditor positions require at least a bachelor's degree in accounting or a related field. Based on recommendations made by the American Institute of Certified Public Accountants, a small number of States currently require CPA candidates to complete 150 semester hours of college coursework—an additional 30 hours beyond the usual four-year bachelor's degree—and many more states are expected to introduce this requirement in the future. Most schools have altered their curricula accordingly, and prospective accounting majors should carefully research accounting curricula and the requirements for any States in which they hope to become licensed before enrolling. Some employers prefer applicants with a master's degree in accounting, or a master's degree in business administration with a concentration in accounting. Most employers also prefer applicants who are familiar with computers and their applications in accounting and internal auditing.

For beginning accounting and auditing positions in the Federal Government, four years of college (including 24 semester hours in accounting or auditing) or an equivalent combination of education and experience is required.

Previous experience in accounting or auditing can help an applicant get a job. Many colleges offer students an opportunity to gain experience through summer or part-time internship programs conducted by public accounting or business firms. Such training is advantageous in gaining permanent employment in the field.

Persons planning a career in accounting should have an aptitude for mathematics; be able to analyze, compare, and interpret facts and figures quickly; and make sound judgments based on this knowledge. They must be able to clearly communicate the results of their work, orally and in writing, to clients and management. Accuracy and the ability to handle responsibility with limited supervision are also important. Perhaps most important, because millions of financial statement users rely on their services, accountants and auditors should have high standards of integrity.

Beginning public accountants usually start by assisting with work for several clients. They may advance to positions with more responsibility in one or two years, and to senior positions within another few years. Those who excel may become supervisors, managers, partners, open their own public accounting firms, or transfer to executive positions in management accounting or internal auditing in private firms.

Beginning management accountants often start as cost accountants, junior internal auditors, or as trainees for other accounting positions. As they rise through the organization, they may advance to accounting manager, chief cost accountant, budget director, or manager of internal auditing. Some become controllers, treasurers, financial vice presidents, chief financial officers, or corporation presidents. Many senior corporation executives have a background in accounting, internal auditing, or finance.

Job Outlook

Accountants and auditors who have earned professional recognition through certification or licensure should have the best job prospects. For example, CPA's should continue to enjoy a wide range of job opportunities, especially as more States enact the 150-hour requirement, making it more difficult to obtain this certification. Similarly, Certified

Management Accountants (CMA's) should be in demand as their management advice is increasingly sought. Applicants with a master's degree in accounting, or a master's degree in business administration with a concentration in accounting, may also have an advantage in the job market. Familiarity with accounting and auditing computer software, or expertise in specialized areas such as international business, specific industries, or current legislation, may also be helpful in landing certain accounting and auditing jobs. In addition, employers increasingly seek well-rounded applicants with strong interpersonal and communication skills. Regardless of one's qualifications, however, competition will remain keen for the most prestigious jobs—those with major accounting and business firms.

Employment of accountants and auditors is expected to grow about <u>as fast as the average</u> for all occupations through the year 2006. The need to replace accountants and auditors who retire or transfer to other occupations will produce thousands of additional job openings annually, reflecting the large size of this occupation.

As the economy grows, the number of business establishments increases, requiring more accountants and auditors to set up their books, prepare their taxes, and provide management advice. As these businesses grow, the volume and complexity of information developed by accountants and auditors on costs, expenditures, and taxes will increase as well. More complex requirements for accountants and auditors also arise from changes in legislation related to taxes, financial reporting standards, business investments, mergers, and other financial matters. In addition, businesses will increasingly need quick, accurate, and individually tailored financial information due to the demands of growing international competition.

The changing role of accountants and auditors also will spur job growth. Accountants will perform less auditing work due to potential liability and relatively low profits, and less tax work due to growing competition from tax preparation firms, but they will offer more management and consulting services in response to market demand. Accountants will continue to take on a greater advisory role as they develop more sophisticated and flexible accounting systems, and focus more on analyzing operations rather than just providing financial data. Internal auditors will be increasingly needed to discover and eliminate waste and fraud.

Earnings

According to a salary survey conducted by the National Association of Colleges and Employers, bachelor's degree candidates in accounting received starting offers averaging $29,400/year in 1996. Master's degree candidates in accounting received starting offers averaging $33,000/year.

According to a survey of workplaces in 160 metropolitan areas, accountants with limited experience had median earnings of $26,000 in 1995, with the middle-half earning between $23,300 and $29,400. The most experienced accountants had median earnings of $87,400, with the middle-half earning between $77,600 and $98,000. Public accountants—employed by public accounting firms—with limited experience had median earnings of $29,400, with the middle-half earning between $28,200 and $32,000. The most experienced public accountants had median earnings of $48,700, with the middle-half earning between $44,500 and $54,000. Many owners and partners of firms earned considerably more.

According to a salary survey conducted by Robert Half International, a staffing services firm specializing in accounting and finance, accountants and auditors with up to one year of experience earned between $25,000 and $39,400 in 1997. Those with one to three years of experience earned between $27,000 and $46,600. Senior accountants and auditors earned between $34,300 and $57,800; managers earned between $40,000 and $81,900; and directors of accounting and auditing earned between $54,800 and $109,800 a year. The variation in salaries reflects differences in size of firm, location, level of education, and professional credentials.

In the Federal Government, the starting annual salary for junior accountants and auditors was about $19,500 in 1997. Candidates who had a superior academic record might start at $24,200, while applicants with a master's degree or two years of professional experience might begin at $29,600. Beginning salaries were slightly higher in selected areas where the prevailing local pay level was higher. Accountants employed by the Federal Government in non-supervisory, supervisory, and managerial positions averaged about $54,000 a year in 1997; auditors averaged $57,900.

Related Occupations

Accountants and auditors design internal control systems and analyze financial data.   Others for whom training in accounting is invaluable include appraisers, budget officers, loan officers, financial analysts and managers, bank officers, actuaries, underwriters, tax collectors and revenue agents, FBI special agents, securities sales representatives, and purchasing agents.

Sources of Additional Information

Information about careers in certified public accounting and about CPA standards and examinations may be obtained from:

American Institute of Certified Public Accountants
Harborside Financial Center
201 Plaza III
Jersey City, NJ 07311-3881
Homepage: *http://www.aicpa.org*

Information on careers in management accounting and the CMA designation may be obtained from:

Institute of Management Accountants
10 Paragon Dr.
Montvale, NJ .7645-1760
Homepage: *http://www.imanet.org*

Information on the Accredited in Accountancy/Accredited Business Accountant, Accredited Tax Advisor, or Accredited Tax Preparer designations may be obtained from:

National Society of Accountants and the Accreditation
     Council for Accountancy and Taxation
1010 North Fairfax St.
Alexandria, VA 22314
Homepage: *http://www.nsacct.org*

Information on careers in internal auditing and the Certified Internal Auditor (CIA) designation may be obtained from:

The Institute of Internal Auditors
249 Maitland Ave.
Altamonte Springs, FL 32701-4201
Homepage: *http://www.theiia.org*

For information on accredited programs in accounting and business, contact:

American Assembly of Collegiate Schools of Business
605 Old Ballas Rd., Suite 220
St. Louis, MO 63141
Homepage: *http://www.aacsb.edu*

5.5 Economics

Nature of the Work

Economists study the ways society distributes scarce resources such as land, labor, raw materials, and machinery to produce goods and services. They conduct research, collect and analyze data, monitor economic trends, and develop forecasts. Typical areas of research include such issues as energy costs, inflation, interest rates, imports, or employment levels.

Most economists are concerned with practical applications of economic policy in a particular area. They use their understanding of economic relationships to advise businesses and other organizations, including insurance companies, banks, securities firms, industry and trade associations, labor unions, and government agencies. Economists use mathematical models to develop programs predicting answers to questions such as the nature and length of business cycles, the effects of a specific rate of inflation on the economy, or the effects of tax legislation on unemployment levels.

Economists who work for government agencies may assess economic conditions in the United States or abroad, in order to estimate the economic effects of specific changes in legislation or public policy. They may study areas such as how the dollar's fluctuation against foreign currencies affects import and export levels. The majority of government economists work in the area of agriculture, labor, or quantitative analysis; some economists work in almost every area of government. For example, some economists in the U.S. Department of Commerce study production, distribution, and consumption of commodities produced overseas, while economists employed with the Bureau of Labor Statistics analyze data on the domestic economy such as prices, wages, employment, productivity, and safety and health.

Economists working in State or local government might analyze data on the growth of school-aged populations, prison growth, and employment and unemployment rates, in order to project spending needs for future years.

Working Conditions

Economists have structured work schedules, often working alone, writing reports, preparing statistical charts, and using computers. Some jobs/projects may also require the economists to be an integral part of a research team. Most work under pressure of deadlines and tight schedules, and sometimes must work overtime. Their routine may be interrupted by special requests for data, as well as by the need to attend meetings or conferences; regular travel may be necessary.

Employment

Private industry, particularly economic and marketing research firms, management consulting firms, banks, securities and commodities brokers, and computer and data processing companies, employ about three out of four salaried workers. A wide range of government agencies employ the remainder, primarily in State Governments. The Departments of Labor, Agriculture, and Commerce are the largest Federal employers of economists. A number of economists combine a full-time job in government, academia, or business with part-time or consulting work in another setting.

Employment of economists is concentrated in large cities. Some economists work abroad for companies with major international operations, for U.S. Government agencies, and for international organizations like the World Bank and the United Nations.

Besides the jobs described above, many economists hold economics faculty positions in colleges and universities. Economics faculty members have flexible work schedules, and may divide their time among teaching, research, consulting, and administration.

Training, Other Qualifications, and Advancement

A bachelor's degree with a major in economics is generally not sufficient to obtain positions as economist, but is excellent preparation for many entry-level positions as a research assistant, administrative or management trainee, marketing interviewer, or any of a number of professional sales jobs.

In the Federal Government, candidates for entry-level economist positions must have a bachelor's degree with a minimum of 21 semester hours of economics and 3 hours of statistics, accounting, or calculus. Competition is keen for those positions that require only a bachelor's degree, and additional education or superior academic performance is likely to be required to gain employment.

Economics majors can choose from a variety of courses, ranging from those which are intensely mathematical such as microeconomics, macroeconomics, and econometrics, to more philosophical courses such as the history of economic thought. Because of the importance of quantitative skills to economic researchers, courses in mathematics, statistics, econometrics, sampling theory and survey design, and computer science are extremely helpful.

Aspiring economists should gain experience gathering and analyzing data, conducting interviews or surveys, and writing reports on their findings while in college. This experience can prove invaluable later in obtaining a full-time position in the field, since much of their work, in the beginning, may center on these duties. With experience, economists eventually are assigned their own research projects.

Those considering careers as economists should be able to work accurately because much time is spent on data analysis. Patience and persistence are necessary qualities since economists must spend long hours on independent study and problem solving. Economists must be able to present their findings, both orally and in writing, in a clear, meaningful way.

Job Outlook

Employment of economists is expected to grow about as fast as the average for all occupations through the year 2006. Most job openings, however, are likely to result from the need to replace experienced workers who transfer to other occupations, retire, or leave the labor force for other reasons.

Opportunities for economists should be best in private industry, especially in research, testing, and consulting firms, as more companies contract out for economic research services. Competition, the growing complexity of the global economy, and increased reliance on quantitative methods for analyzing the current value of future funds, business trends, sales, and purchasing should spur demand for economists. The growing need for economic analyses in virtually every industry should result in additional jobs for economists. Employment of economists in the Federal

Government should decline more slowly than the rate projected for the entire Federal workforce. Average employment growth is expected among economists in state and local government.

Graduates with a bachelor's degree in economics through the year 2006 will face keen competition for the limited number of economist positions for which they qualify. However, graduates will qualify for a number of other positions where they can take advantage of their economic knowledge in conducting research, developing surveys, or analyzing data. Many bachelors' degree graduates will find good jobs in industry and business as management trainees, sales trainees, or administrative assistants. Economists with good quantitative skills are qualified for research assistant positions in a broad range of fields. Those who meet State certification requirements may become high school economics teachers. The demand for secondary school economics teachers is expected to grow as economics becomes an increasingly important and popular course.

Earnings

According to a 1997 salary survey by the National Association of Colleges and Employers, persons with a bachelor's degree in economics received offers averaging $31,300 a year. The median base salary of business economists in 1996 was $73,000, according to a survey by the National Association of Business Economists. The median entry-level salary was about $35,000, with most new entrants' possessing a masters degree.

The Federal Government recognizes education and experience in certifying applicants for entry-level positions. The entrance salary for economists having a bachelor's degree was about $19,500 a year in 1997. However, those with superior academic records could begin at $24,200. Those having a master's degree could qualify for positions at an annual salary of $29,600. Those with a Ph.D. could begin at $35,800, while some individuals with experience and an advanced degree could start at $42,900. Starting salaries were slightly higher in selected areas where the prevailing local pay was higher. The average annual salary for economists employed by the Federal Government was $63,870 a year in early 1997.

Related Occupations

Economists are concerned with understanding and interpreting financial matters, among other subjects. Other jobs in this area include financial managers, financial analysts, underwriters, actuaries, credit analysts, loan officers, and budget officers.

Sources of Additional Information

For information on careers in economics and business, contact:

> National Association of Business Economists
> 1233 20th St. NW, Suite 505
> Washington, DC 20036
>
> Homepage: *http://www.nabe.com/members.htm*

For information on obtaining a job with the Federal Government, contact the Office of Personnel Management through a telephone-based system. Consult your telephone directory under U.S. Government for a local number or call: (912) 757-3000. The number is not toll-free, and charges may result. Information also is available from their Internet site: *http://www.usajobs.opm.gov/*

5.6 Finance

Nature of the Work

Practically every firm has one or more financial managers. Among them are chief financial officers, vice presidents of finance, treasurers, controllers, credit managers, and cash managers; they prepare the financial reports required by the firm to conduct its operations and to ensure that the firm satisfies tax and regulatory requirements. Financial managers also oversee the flow of cash and financial instruments, monitor the extension of credit, assess the risk of transactions, raise capital, analyze investments, develop information to assess the present and future financial status of the firm, and communicate with stock holders and other investors.

In small firms, chief financial officers usually handle all financial management functions. In large firms, these officers oversee financial management departments and help top managers develop financial and economic policy, establish procedures, delegate authority, and oversee the implementation of these policies.

Financial institutions—such as banks, savings and loan associations, credit unions, personal credit institutions, and finance companies—may serve as depositories for cash and financial instruments and offer loans, investment counseling, consumer credit, trust management, and other financial services. Some specialize in specific financial services. Financial managers in financial institutions include vice presidents, bank branch managers, savings and loan association managers, consumer credit managers, and credit union managers. These managers make decisions in accordance with policy set by the institution's board of directors and Federal and State laws and regulations.

Due to changing regulations and increased government scrutiny, financial managers in financial institutions must place greater emphasis on accurate reporting of financial data. They must have detailed knowledge of industries allied to banking—such as insurance, real estate, and securities—and a broad knowledge of business and industrial activities. With growing domestic and foreign competition, financial managers must keep abreast of an expanding and increasingly complex variety of financial products and services. Besides supervising financial services, financial managers in banks and other financial institutions may advise individuals and businesses on financial planning.

Working Conditions

Financial managers are provided with comfortable offices, often close to top managers and to departments that develop the financial data these managers need. Financial managers typically work 40 hours a week, but many work longer hours. They are often required to attend meetings of financial and economic associations, and may travel to visit subsidiary firms or meet customers.

Employment

Financial managers held about 800,000 jobs in 1996. Although these managers are found in virtually every industry, more than a third were employed by service industries, including business, health, social, and management services. Nearly 3 out of 10 were employed by financial institutions—banks, savings institutions, finance companies, credit unions, insurance companies, securities dealers, and real estate firms, for example.

Training, Other Qualifications, and Advancement

A bachelor's degree in finance, accounting, economics, or business administration is the minimum academic preparation for financial managers. However, many employers increasingly seek graduates with a master's degree, preferably in business administration, economics, finance, or risk management. These academic programs develop analytical skills, and provide knowledge of the latest financial analysis methods and information and technology management techniques widely used in this field.

Experience may be more important than formal education for some financial manager positions—notably branch managers in banks. Banks typically fill branch manager positions by promoting experienced loan officers and other professionals who excel at their jobs.

Continuing education is vital for financial managers, reflecting the growing complexity of global trade, shifting Federal and State laws and regulations, and a proliferation of new, complex financial instruments. Firms often provide opportunities for workers to broaden their knowledge and skills, and encourage employees to take graduate courses at colleges and universities or attend conferences relating to their specialty.

Financial management, banking, and credit union associations, often in cooperation with colleges and universities, sponsor numerous national or local training programs. In some cases, financial managers may also broaden their skills and exhibit their competency in specialized fields by attaining professional certification. For example, the Association for Investment Management and Research confers the Chartered Financial Analyst designation to investment professionals who have a bachelor's degree, pass three test levels, and meet work experience requirements. The National Association of Credit Management administers a three-part certification program for business credit professionals. Through a combination of experience and examinations, these financial managers pass through the level of Credit Business Associate, to Credit Business Fellow, to Certified Credit Executive. The Treasury Management Association confers the Certified Cash Manager credential on those who have two years of relevant experience and pass an exam, and the Certified Treasury Executive designation on those more senior in treasury management who meet experience and continuing education requirements.

Persons interested in becoming financial managers should enjoy working independently, dealing with people, and analyzing detailed account information. The ability to communicate effectively, both orally and in writing is also important. They also need tact, good judgment, and the ability to establish effective personal relationships to oversee staff.

Job Outlook

Like other managerial occupations, the number of applicants for financial management positions is expected to exceed the number of openings, resulting in competition for jobs. Those with lending experience, and familiarity with the latest lending regulations and financial products and services, should enjoy the best opportunities for branch management jobs in banks. Those with a graduate degree, a strong analytical background, and knowledge of various aspects of financial management, such as asset management and information and technology management, should enjoy the best opportunities for other financial management positions. Developing expertise in a rapidly growing industry, such as health care, could also be an advantage in the job market.

Employment of financial managers is expected to increase about as fast as the average for all occupations through the year 2006. The need for skilled financial management will increase due to the demands of global trade, the proliferation of complex financial instruments, and changing Federal and State laws and regulations. Many firms have reduced the ranks of middle managers in an effort to be more efficient and competitive, but much of the downsizing and restructuring is complete. The banking industry, on the other hand, is still undergoing mergers and consolidation, and may eliminate some financial management positions as a result.

Earnings

The median annual salary of financial managers was $40,700 in 1996. The lowest 10 percent earned $21,800 or less, while the top 10 percent earned over $81,100.

According to a 1997 survey by Robert Half International, a staffing services firm specializing in accounting and finance, salaries of assistant controllers range from $41,000 in the smallest firms, to $81,000 in the largest firms; controllers, $47,000 to $138,000; and chief financial officers/treasurers, $62,000 to $307,000.

The results of the Treasury Management Association's 1997 compensation survey are presented in Table 1. The earnings listed in the table represent total compensation, including bonuses. The survey also found that financial managers with a master's degree in business administration average $10,900 more than managers with a bachelor's degree.

Table 1
Annual earnings for selected 1997 financial managers

Title	Earning
Chief financial officer	$142,900
Vice president of finance	138,000
Treasurer	122,500
Assistant treasurer	88,400
Controller	85,100
Treasury manager	66,900
Assistant controller	56,200
Senior analyst	55,600
Cash manager	51,600
Analyst	40,500
Assistant cash manager	38,800

SOURCE: Treasury Management Association

Related Occupations

Financial managers combine formal education with experience in one or more areas of finance, such as asset management, lending, credit operations, securities investment, or insurance risk and loss control. Workers in other occupations requiring similar training and ability include accountants and auditors, budget officers, credit analysts, loan officers, insurance consultants, portfolio managers, pension consultants, real estate advisors, securities analysts and underwriters.

Sources of Additional Information

For information about financial management careers contact:

American Bankers Association
1120 Connecticut Ave. NW.
Washington, DC 20036

Homepage:
http://www.aba.com/abatool/showme_rel.html?location=homepage

For information about financial careers in business credit management; the Credit Business Associate, Credit Business Fellow, and Certified Credit Executive programs; and institutions offering graduate courses in credit and financial management, contact:

National Association of Credit Management (NACM)
Credit Research Foundation
8815 Centre Park Dr.
Columbia, MD 21045-2117
Homepage: *http://www.nacm.org/*

For information about careers in treasury management from entry level to chief financial officer, and the Certified Cash Manager and Certified Treasury Executive programs, contact:

Treasury Management Association
7315 Wisconsin Ave., Suite 600 West
Bethesda, MD 20814.

Homepage: *http://www.tma-net.org/aboutmem/index.html*

5.7 Management (Organizational Behavior)

Nature of the Work

Administrative services managers are employed throughout the American economy, and their range of duties is broad. They coordinate and direct support services, which may include: secretarial and reception; administration; payroll; conference planning and travel; information and data processing; mail; facilities management; materials scheduling and distribution; printing and reproduction; records management; telecommunications management; personal property procurement, supply, and disposal; security; and parking

In small organizations, a single administrative service manager may oversee all support services. In larger ones, however, first-line administrative service managers report to mid-level supervisors who, in turn, report to proprietors or top-level managers. First-line administrative service managers directly oversee a staff that performs various support services. Mid-level managers develop departmental plans, set goals and deadlines, develop procedures to improve productivity and customer service, and define the responsibilities of supervisory-level managers. They are often involved in the hiring and dismissal of employees, but generally have no role in the formulation of personnel policy.

Working Conditions

Administrative service managers generally work in comfortable offices. In smaller organizations, they may work alongside the people they supervise and the office may be crowded and noisy.

The work of administrative service managers can be stressful, as they attempt to schedule work to meet deadlines. Although the 40-hour week is standard, uncompensated overtime is often required to resolve problems. Managers involved in personal property procurement, use, and disposal may travel extensively between their home office, branch offices, vendors' offices, and property sales sites. Facilities managers who are responsible for the design of workspaces may spend time at construction sites and may travel between different facilities while monitoring the work of maintenance, grounds, and custodial staffs.

Employment

Administrative service managers held about 291,000 jobs in 1996. Over one-half worked in service industries, including management, business, social, and health services organizations. Others were found in virtually every other industry.

Training, Other Qualifications, and Advancement

Many administrative service managers advance through the ranks in their organization, acquiring work experience in various administrative positions before assuming first-line supervisory duties. All managers who oversee departmental supervisors should be familiar with office procedures and equipment. Facilities managers may have a background in architecture, engineering, construction, interior design, or real estate, in addition to managerial experience. Managers of personal property acquisition and disposal need experience in purchasing and sales, and knowledge of a wide variety of supplies, machinery, and equipment. Managers concerned with supply, inventory, and distribution must be experienced in receiving, warehousing, packaging, shipping, transportation, and related operations. Managers of unclaimed property often have experience in insurance claims analysis and records management.

For first-line administrative service managers of secretarial, mailroom, and related support activities, many employers prefer an associate degree in business or management, although a high school diploma may suffice when combined with appropriate experience. For managers of audiovisual, graphics, and other technical activities, postsecondary technical school training is preferred. For managers of highly complex services, a bachelor's degree in business, human resources, or finance is often required. The curriculum should include courses in office technology, accounting, business mathematics, computer applications, human resources, and business law.

Persons interested in becoming administrative service managers should have good communication skills and be able to establish effective working relationships with many different people, ranging from managers, supervisors, and professionals, to clerks and blue-collar workers. They should be analytical, detail oriented, flexible, and decisive. The ability to coordinate several activities at once and quickly analyze and resolve specific problems is important. Ability to work under pressure and cope with deadlines is also important.

Job Outlook

Employment of administrative service managers is expected to grow about as fast as the average for all occupations through the year 2006. Like other managerial occupations, this occupation is characterized by low turnover. These factors, coupled with the ample supply of competent, experienced workers seeking managerial jobs, should result in keen competition for administrative services management positions.

Many firms are increasingly contracting out administrative service positions and otherwise streamlining these functions in an effort to cut costs. Corporate restructuring has reduced the number of administrative service manager positions, and this trend is expected to continue.

As it becomes more common for firms and governments at all levels to contract out administrative services, demand for administrative services managers will increase in the management services, management consulting, and facilities support services firms providing these services.

Earnings

Earnings of administrative service managers vary greatly depending on their employer, specialty, and geographic area in which they work. According to a 1996 survey conducted by the AMS Foundation, building services/facilities managers earned about $53,800 a year in 1996; office/administrative services managers earned about $41,400; and records managers about $37,900.

In the Federal Government, facilities managers in non-supervisory, supervisory, and managerial positions averaged $49,140 a year in early 1997; miscellaneous administrative and program officers, $53,330; industrial property managers, $47,930; property disposal specialists, $43,460; administrative officers $49,070, and support services administrators, $39,700.

Related Occupations

Administrative services managers direct and coordinate support services and oversee the purchase, use, and disposal of personal property. Occupations with similar functions include administrative assistants, appraisers, buyers, clerical supervisors, contract specialists, cost estimators, procurement services managers, property and real estate managers, purchasing managers, and personnel managers.

Sources of Additional Information

For information about careers in facilities management, contact:

International Facility Management Association
1 East Greenway Plaza, Suite 1100
Houston, TX 77046-0194
Homepage: *http://www.ifmahouston.org/*

5.8 *Management Information Systems*

Nature of the Work

Computer systems managers plan, coordinate, and direct research, development, design, production, and computer-related activities. They supervise a staff, which may include engineers, scientists, technicians, computer specialists, and information technology workers, along with support personnel.

Computer systems managers determine scientific and technical goals within broad outlines provided by top management. These goals may include the redesigning of an aircraft, improvements in manufacturing processes, the development of a large computer program, or advances in scientific research. Managers make detailed plans for the accomplishment of these goals. For example, working with their staff, they may develop the overall concepts of new products or identify problems standing in the way of project completion. They determine the cost of and equipment and personnel needed for projects and programs. They hire and assign scientists, engineers, technicians, computer specialists, information technology workers, and support personnel to carry out specific parts of the projects. The managers supervise these employees' work, and review their designs, programs, and reports. They present ideas and projects to top management for approval or when seeking additional funds for development.

Computer systems managers direct and plan programming, computer operations, and data processing, and coordinate the development of computer hardware, systems design, and software. Top-level managers direct all computer-related activities in an organization. They analyze the computer and data information requirements of their organization and assign, schedule, and review the work of systems analysts, computer programmers, and computer operators. They determine personnel and computer hardware requirements, evaluate equipment options, and make purchasing decisions.

Working Conditions

Computer systems managers spend most of their time in an office. Some managers, however, may also work in laboratories or industrial plants and may occasionally be exposed to the same conditions as production workers. Most managers work at least 40 hours a week and may work much longer on occasion if meeting project deadlines. Some may experience considerable pressure in meeting technical or scientific goals within a short time or a tight budget.

Employment

Computer, engineering, and science systems managers held about 343,000 jobs in 1996. Although these managers are found in almost all industries, about 38 percent are employed in manufacturing, especially in the industrial machinery and equipment, electrical and electronic equipment, instruments, chemicals, and transportation equipment industries. However, the two industries employing the greatest number of these managers were engineering and architectural services and computer and data processing services; each employed about one in ten in 1996. Others work for government agencies, research and testing services, communications and utilities companies, financial and insurance firms, and management and public relations services companies.

Training, Other Qualifications, and Advancement

It is essential that computer systems managers have a base of technical knowledge that allows them to understand and guide the work of their subordinates and to explain the work in non-technical terms to senior management and potential customers. Therefore, experience as a computer professional is usually required to become a computer systems manager. Educational requirements are consequently similar to those for computer professionals.

Most computer systems managers have been systems analysts, although some may have experience as computer engineers, programmers, operators, or other computer specialties. There is no universally accepted way of preparing for a job as a systems analyst. Many have degrees in computer or information science, computer information systems, or data processing and have experience as computer programmers. A bachelor's degree is usually required and employers often prefer a graduate degree. A typical career advancement progression in a large organization would be from programmer to programmer/analyst, to systems analyst, and then to project leader or senior analyst. The first real managerial position might be as project manager, programming supervisor, systems supervisor, or software manager.

In addition to educational requirements computer specialists must demonstrate above average technical skills to be considered for a promotion to manager. Employers also look for leadership and communication skills, as well as managerial attributes such as the ability to make rational decisions, to manage time well, organize and coordinate work effectively, establish good working and personal relationships, and motivate others. A successful manager must also have the desire to perform management functions. Many computer specialists want to be promoted but actually prefer doing technical work.

Job Outlook

Employment of computer, engineering, and science systems managers is expected to increase much faster than the average for all occupations through the year 2006. Employment of computer systems managers will increase rapidly due to the fast-paced expansion of the computer and data processing services industry and the increased employment of computer systems analysts. Large computer centers are consolidating or closing as small computers become more powerful, resulting in fewer opportunities for computer systems managers at these centers. However, as the economy expands and as advances in technology lead to broader applications for computers, opportunities will increase and employment should grow rapidly.

Opportunities for those who wish to become computer systems managers should be closely related to the growth of the occupations they supervise and the industries in which they are found. Because computer specialists are eligible for management and seek promotion, there may be substantial competition for these openings.

Earnings

Earnings for computer systems managers vary by specialty and level of management. According to Robert Half International, computer systems managers earned salaries ranging from $33,000 to well over $100,000, depending on establishment size. Managers often earn about 15 to 25 percent more than those they directly supervise, although there are cases in which some employees are paid more than the manager who supervises them. This is especially true in research fields.

According to a survey of workplaces in 160 metropolitan areas, beginning systems analysts managers had median annual earnings of $60,900, with the middle-half earning between $55,100 and $67,000. The most senior systems analysts managers had median annual earnings of $84,200, with the middle-half earning between $76,200 and $92,000.

In addition, computer systems managers, especially those at higher levels, often are provided with more benefits (such as expense accounts, stock option plans, and bonuses) than non-managerial workers in their organizations.

Related Occupations

The work of computer systems managers is closely related to that of computer personnel. It is also related to the work of other managers, *especially general managers and top executives.*

Sources of Additional Information

For information about certification as a computing professional, contact:

Institute for Certification of Computing Professionals (ICCP)
2200 East Devon Ave., Suite 268
Des Plaines, IL 60018
Homepage: ***http://www.iccp.org***

Further information about computer careers is available from:

The Association for Computing (ACM)
1515 Broadway
New York, NY 10036

Homepage: ***http://www.acm.org/cacm/careeropps/***

or

IEEE Computer Society
Headquarters Office
1730 Massachusetts Ave, NW
Washington, DC 20036-1992

Homepage: ***http://www.ieee.org/eab/***

5.9 Marketing

Nature of the Work

Marketing managers develop the firm's detailed marketing strategy. With the help of subordinates, including product development managers and market research managers, they determine the demand for products and services offered by the firm and its competitors and identify potential consumers. Marketing managers develop pricing strategy with an eye toward maximizing the firm's share of the market and its profits while ensuring that the firm's customers are satisfied. In collaboration with sales, product development, and other managers, they monitor trends that indicate the need for new products and services and oversee product development

Sales managers direct the firm's sales program. They assign sales territories and goals and establish training programs for their sales representatives. Managers advise their sales representatives on ways to improve their sales performance. In large, multi-product firms, they oversee regional and local sales managers and their staffs. Sales managers maintain contact with dealers and distributors. They analyze sales statistics gathered by their staffs to determine sales potential and inventory requirements and monitor the preferences of customers. Such information is vital to develop products and maximize profits.

Advertising managers oversee the account services, creative services, and media services departments. The account services department is managed by account executives, who assess the need for advertising and, in advertising agencies, maintain the accounts of clients. The creative services department develops the subject matter and presentation of advertising. A creative director, who oversees the copy chief and art director and their staffs, supervises this department. The media services department is supervised by the media director, who oversees planning groups that select the communication media—for example, radio, television, newspapers, magazines, or outdoor signs—to disseminate the advertising.

Promotion managers supervise staffs of promotion specialists. They direct promotion programs combining advertising with purchase incentives to increase sales. In an effort to establish closer contact with purchasers—dealers, distributors, or consumers—promotion programs may involve direct mail, telemarketing, television or radio advertising, catalogs, exhibits, inserts in newspapers, in-store displays and product endorsements, and special events.

Public relations managers direct publicity programs to a targeted public. They use any necessary communication media in their effort to maintain the support of the specific group upon whom their organization's success depends, such as consumers, stockholders, or the general public. They evaluate advertising and promotion programs for compatibility with public relations efforts, and, in effect, serve as the eyes and ears of top management. They observe social, economic, and political trends that might ultimately have an effect upon the firm, and make recommendations to enhance the firm's image based on those trends.

Working Conditions

Marketing, advertising, and public relations managers are provided with offices close to top managers. Long hours, including evenings and weekends, are common. Almost 45 percent of marketing, advertising, and public relations managers worked 50 hours or more a week, compared to 20 percent for all occupations. Working under pressure is unavoidable as schedules change, problems arise, and deadlines and goals must be met.

Marketing, advertising, and public relations managers meet frequently with other managers; some meet with the public and government officials.

Substantial travel may be involved. For example, attendance at meetings sponsored by associations or industries is often mandatory. Sales managers travel to national, regional, and local offices and to various dealers and distributors. Advertising and promotion managers may travel to meet with clients or representatives of communications media. At times, public relations managers travel to meet with special interest groups or government officials. Job transfers between headquarters and regional offices are common—particularly among sales managers—and can disrupt family life.

Employment

Marketing, advertising, and public relations managers held about 482,000 jobs in 1996. They are found in virtually every industry. Industries employing them in significant numbers include motor vehicle dealers, printing and publishing, advertising, department stores, computer and data processing services, and management and public relations.

Training, Other Qualifications, and Advancement

A wide range of educational backgrounds is suitable for entry into marketing, advertising, and public relations managerial jobs, but many employers prefer a broad liberal arts background. A bachelor's degree in sociology, psychology, literature, or philosophy, among other subjects, is acceptable. However, requirements vary depending upon the particular job.

For marketing, sales, and promotion management positions, some employers prefer a bachelors or master's degree in business administration with an emphasis on marketing. Courses in business law, economics, accounting, finance, mathematics, and statistics are also highly recommended. For advertising management positions, some employers prefer a bachelor's degree in advertising or journalism. A course of study should include courses in marketing, consumer behavior, market research, sales, communications methods and technology, and visual arts—for example, art history and photography. For public relations management positions, some employers prefer a bachelors or master's degree in public relations or journalism. The individual's curriculum should include courses in advertising, business administration, public affairs, political science, and creative and technical writing. For all these specialties, courses in management and completion of an internship while in school are highly recommended. Familiarity with word processing and database applications also is important for many marketing, advertising, and public relations management positions.

Persons interested in becoming marketing, advertising, and public relations managers should be mature, creative, highly motivated, resistant to stress, and flexible, yet decisive. The ability to communicate persuasively, both orally and in writing, with other managers, staff, and the public is vital. Marketing, advertising, and public relations managers also need tact, good judgment, and exceptional ability to establish and maintain effective personal relationships with supervisory and professional staff members and client firms.

Job Outlook

Marketing, advertising, and public relations manager jobs are highly coveted and will be sought by other managers or highly experienced professional and technical personnel, resulting in substantial job competition. College graduates with extensive experience, a high level of creativity, and strong communication skills should have the best job opportunities. Those who have new media and interactive marketing skills will be particularly sought after.

Employment of marketing, advertising, and public relations managers is expected to increase faster than the average for all occupations through the year 2006. Increasingly intense domestic and global competition in products and services offered to consumers should require greater marketing, promotional, and public relations efforts by managers. Management and public relations firms may experience particularly rapid growth as businesses increasingly hire contractors for these services rather than support additional full-time staff.

Projected employment growth varies by industry. For example, employment of marketing, advertising, and public relations managers is expected to grow much faster than average in most business services industries, such as computer and data processing, and management and public relations firms, while average growth is projected in manufacturing industries overall.

Earnings

According to a National Association of Colleges and Employers survey, starting salaries for marketing majors graduating in 1997 averaged about $29,000; advertising majors, about $27,000.

The median annual salary of marketing, advertising, and public relations managers was $46,000 in 1996. The lowest 10 percent earned $23,000 or less, while the top 10 percent earned $97,000 or more. Many earn bonuses equal to 10 percent or more of their salaries. Surveys show that salary levels vary substantially depending upon the level of managerial responsibility, length of service, education, and the employer's size, location, and industry. For example, manufacturing firms generally pay marketing, advertising, and public relations managers higher salaries than non-manufacturing firms do. For sales managers, the size of their sales territory is another important determinant of salary.

According to a 1996 survey by *Advertising Age Magazine*, the average annual salary of a vice president brand manager was $79,000; vice president product manager, $105,000; vice president advertising, $130,000; and vice president marketing, $133,000. According to a 1996 survey by the Public Relations Society of America, senior public relations managers earned an average of $76,790.

Related Occupations

Marketing, advertising, and public relations managers direct the sale of products and services offered by their firms and the communication of information about their firms' activities. Other personnel involved with marketing, advertising, and public relations include art directors, commercial and graphic artists, copy chiefs, copywriters, lobbyists, marketing research analysts, public relations specialists, promotion specialists, sales representatives, editors and technical writers.

Sources of Additional Information

For information about careers in sales and marketing management, contact:

American Marketing Association
250 S. Wacker Dr.
Chicago, IL 60606.

Homepage: *http://www.chicagoama.org/index.html*

For information about careers in advertising management, contact:

American Advertising Federation
Education Services Department
1101 Vermont Ave. NW, Suite 500
Washington, DC 20005

Homepage: *http://www.aaf.org/*

Information about careers in public relations management is available from:

Public Relations Society of America
33 Irving Place
New York, NY 10003-2376

Homepage: *http://www.prsa.org/*

Information on accreditation for business communicators is available from:

International Association of Business Communicators
One Hallidie Plaza, Suite 600
San Francisco, CA 94102.

Job Line Page: *http://www.iabc.com/~seattle/index.html*

5.10 General Business Administration Career Opportunities

There are many opportunities available to business graduates that do not require a specific business major. The business graduate possesses the appropriate academic background to effectively compete for these opportunities. I have selected five career fields:

Budget Analyst

Management Analyst

Loan Officer

Production Manager

Human Resource Manager

This will provide you with a sampling of the many opportunities your business degree can offer you.

Budget Analyst

Nature of the Work.

Budget analysts play a primary role in the development, analysis, and execution of budgets. Budgets are financial plans used to estimate future requirements and organize and allocate operating and capital resources effectively. The analysis of spending behavior and the planning of future operations are an integral part of the decision-making process in most corporations and government agencies.

Budget analysts work in private industry, nonprofit organizations, and the public sector. In private industry, a budget analyst examines, analyzes, and seeks new ways to improve efficiency and increase profits. Although analysts working in government generally are not concerned with profits, they too are interested in finding the most efficient distribution of funds and other resources among various departments and programs.

A major responsibility of budget analysts is to provide advice and technical assistance in the preparation of annual budgets. At the beginning of the budget cycle, managers and department heads submit proposed operating and financial plans to budget analysts for review. These plans outline expected programs, including proposed program increases and new initiatives, estimated costs and expenses, and capital expenditures needed to finance these programs.

Working Conditions.

Budget analysts work in a normal office setting, generally 40 hours per week. However, during the initial development and mid-year and final reviews of budgets, they often experience the pressure of deadlines and tight work schedules. The work during these periods can be extremely stressful, and analysts are usually required to work more than the routine 40 hours a week.

Budget analysts spend the majority of their time working independently, compiling and analyzing data and preparing budget proposals. Nevertheless, their routine schedule can be interrupted by special budget requests, meetings, and training sessions. Others may travel to obtain budget details and explanations of various programs from coworkers, and to personally observe what funding is being used for in the field.

Employment.

Budget analysts held about 66,000 jobs throughout private industry and government in 1996. Federal, state, and local governments are major employers, accounting for one-third of budget analyst jobs. The Department of Defense employed seven of every ten budget analysts working for the Federal Government. Other major employers of budget analysts are schools, hospitals, banks; and manufacturers of transportation equipment, chemicals and allied products, electrical and electronic machinery, and industrial machines.

Training, Other Qualifications, and Advancement.

Private firms and government agencies generally require candidates for budget analyst positions to have at least a bachelor's degree. Within the Federal Government, a bachelor's degree in any field is sufficient background for an entry-level budget analyst position. State and local governments have varying requirements, but a bachelor's degree in one of many areas—accounting, finance, business or public administration, economics, political science, planning, statistics, or a social science such as sociology—may qualify one for entry into the occupation. Because developing a budget involves manipulating numbers and requires strong analytical skills, courses in statistics or accounting are helpful, regardless of the prospective budget analyst's major field of study. Financial analysis in most organizations is automated, and requires familiarity with word processing and the financial software packages used in budget analysis. Employers generally prefer job candidates who already possess these computer skills over those who need to be trained.

In addition to analytical and computer skills, those seeking a career as a budget analyst must also be able to work under strict time constraints. Strong oral and written communication skills are essential for analysts to prepare, present, and defend budget proposals to decision-makers.

In the Federal Government beginning budget analysts compare projected costs with prior expenditures, consolidate and enter data prepared by others, and assist higher-grade analysts by doing research. As analysts progress, they begin to develop and formulate budget estimates and justification statements, perform in-depth analyses of budget requests, write statements supporting funding requests, advise program managers and others on the status and availability of funds in different budget activities, and present and defend budget proposals to senior managers.

Job Outlook.

Despite the increase in demand for budget analysts, competition for jobs should remain keen because of the substantial number of qualified applicants. Job opportunities are generally best for candidates with a master's degree. In some cases, budget and financial experience can offset a lack of formal education. A working knowledge of computer financial software packages can also enhance one's employment prospects in this field.

Employment of budget analysts is expected to grow about as fast as the average for all occupations through the year 2006. In addition to employment growth, many job openings will result from the need to replace experienced budget analysts who transfer to other occupations or leave the labor force.

Planning and financial control demand more attention because of the growing complexity of business and the increasing specialization within organizations. Many companies will continue to rely heavily on budget analysts to examine, analyze, and develop budgets to determine capital requirements and to allocate labor and other resources efficiently among all parts of the organization. Managers will continue to use budgets as a vehicle to plan, coordinate, control, and evaluate activities within their organizations more effectively.

Earnings.

Salaries of budget analysts vary widely by experience, education, and employer. According to a survey conducted by Robert Half International, a staffing services firm specializing in accounting and finance, starting salaries of budget and other financial analysts in small firms ranged from $24,000 to $33,200 in 1997; in large organizations, from $28,000 to $38,700. In small firms, analysts with one to three years of experience earned from $28,000 to $43,100; in large companies, from $31,000 to $51,300. Senior analysts in small firms earned from $34,500 to $50,000; in large firms, from $39,000 to $60,600. Earnings of managers in this field ranged from $40,000 to $65,000 a year in small firms, while managers in large organizations earned between $47,000 and $83,800.

A survey of workplaces in 160 metropolitan areas reported that inexperienced budget analysts had median annual earnings of about

$30,100 in 1995, with the middle-half earning between $26,200 and $35,500 a year.

In the Federal Government, budget analysts generally started as trainees earning $19,500 or $24,200 a year in 1997. Candidates with a master's degree might begin at $29,600. Beginning salaries were slightly higher in selected areas where the prevailing local pay level was higher. The average annual salary for budget analysts employed by the Federal Government in non-supervisory, supervisory, and managerial positions was $48,600 in 1997.

Related Occupations.

Budget analysts review, analyze, and interpret financial data; make recommendations for the future; and assist in the implementation of new ideas. Workers who use these skills in other occupations include accountants and auditors, economists, financial analysts, financial managers, and loan officers.

Sources of Additional Information.

Information on acquiring a job as a budget analyst with the Federal Government may be obtained from the Office of Personnel Management through a telephone-based system. Consult your telephone directory under U.S. Government for a local number, or call (912) 757-3000. That number is not toll-free and charges may result. Information also is available from their Internet site: *http://www.usajobs.opm.gov.*

Management Analyst

Nature of the Work.

Management analysts and consultants analyze and suggest solutions to management problems. For example, a rapidly growing small company may need help in designing a better system of control over inventories and expenses and decides to engage a consultant who is an expert in just-in-time inventory management.

The work of management analysts and consultants varies with each client or employer and from project to project. For example, some projects require a team of consultants, each specializing in one area; at other times, consultants work independently with the organization's managers. In general, analysts and consultants collect, review, and analyze information. They then make recommendations to management and may assist in the implementation of their proposal.

Both public and private organizations use consultants for a variety of reasons. Some don't have the internal resources needed to handle a project, while others need a consultant's expertise to determine what resources will be required, and what problems may be encountered, if they pursue a particular opportunity. Firms providing consulting services range in size from a single practitioner to large international organizations employing many thousands of consultants. Some analysts and consultants specialize in a specific industry while others specialize by type of business function, such as human resources or information systems. In government, management analysts tend to specialize by type of agency.

Working Conditions.

Management analysts and consultants usually divide their time between their offices and their client's site. Although much of their time is spent indoors in clean, well-lighted offices, they may experience a great deal of stress as a result of trying to meet a client's demands, often on a tight schedule.

Typically, analysts and consultants work at least 40 hours a week. Uncompensated overtime is common, especially when project deadlines are near. Since they must spend a significant portion of their time with clients, they travel frequently.

Self-employed consultants can set their workload and hours and work at home. On the other hand, their livelihood depends on their ability to maintain and expand their client base. Salaried consultants also must impress potential clients to get and keep clients for their company.

Employment.

Management analysts and consultants held about 244,000 jobs in 1996. Around 45 percent of these workers were self-employed. Most of the rest worked in financial and management consulting firms and for Federal, State, and local governments. The majority of those working for the Federal Government were found in the Department of Defense.

Management analysts and consultants are found throughout the country, but employment is concentrated in large metropolitan areas.

Training, Other Qualifications, and Advancement.

Educational requirements for entry-level jobs in this field vary widely between private industry and government. Employers in private industry generally seek individuals with a master's degree in business administration or a related discipline and at least five years of experience in the field in which they hope to consult. Most government agencies hire people with a bachelor's degree and no work experience as entry-level management analysts.

Many fields of study provide a suitable educational background for this occupation because of the wide range of problem areas addressed by management analysts and consultants. These include most areas of business and management. Most entrants to this occupation have, in addition to the appropriate formal education, years of experience in management, human resources, inventory control, or other specialties. The value of this experience enables many to land consultant positions, since most prospective clients now demand experience in the area where they feel they need help.

Management analysts and consultants often work with little or no supervision, so they should be self-motivated and disciplined. Analytical skills, the ability to get along with a wide range of people, strong oral and written communication skills, good judgment, the ability to manage time well, and creativity in developing solutions to problems are other desirable qualities for prospective management analysts and consultants.

Job Outlook.

Employment of management analysts and consultants is expected to grow faster than the average for all occupations through the year 2006 as industry and government increasingly relies on outside expertise to improve the performance of their organizations. Growth is expected in very large consulting firms, but also in smaller niche consulting firms whose consultants specialize in specific areas of expertise. For example, some consultants specialize in biotechnology, pharmacy, engineering, or telecommunications. Clients increasingly demand a team approach, which enables examination of a variety of different areas within the organization. This development may hinder individual practitioners.

Management consultants are being increasingly relied upon to help reduce costs, streamline operations, and develop marketing strategies. As businesses downsize, opportunities will be created for consultants to perform duties that were previously handled internally. Businesses attempting to expand, particularly into world markets, frequently need the skills of management consultants to help with organizational, administrative, and other issues. Continuing changes in the business environment also are expected to lead the demand for consultants to incorporate new technologies, and to adapt to a changing labor force.

Federal, state, and local agencies also are expected to expand their use of management analysts. Analysts' skills at identifying problems and implementing cost reduction measures are expected to become increasingly important.

Despite projected rapid employment growth, competition for jobs as management analysts and consultants is expected to be keen. Because management consultants can come from diverse educational backgrounds, the pool of applicants from which employers can hire is quite large. Additionally, the independent and challenging nature of the work, combined with high earnings potential, make this occupation attractive to many. Job opportunities are expected to be best for those with a graduate degree, a talent for salesmanship and public relations, and industry expertise.

Earnings.

Salaries for management analysts and consultants vary widely by experience, education, and employer. In 1996, those who were full-time wage and salary workers had median annual earnings of about $39,500. The middle 50 percent earned between $30,200 and $61,300, and the top 10 percent earned more than $81,500.

In 1996, according to the Association of Management Consulting Firms, earnings—including bonuses and/or profit sharing—for research associates in member firms averaged $32,400; for entry level consultants, $35,200; for management consultants, $50,500; for senior consultants, $74,300; for junior partners, $91,100; and for senior partners, $167,100.

The average annual salary for management analysts in the Federal Government in non-supervisory, supervisory, and managerial positions was $55,240 in 1997.

Typical benefits for salaried analysts and consultants include health and life insurance, a retirement plan, vacation and sick leave, profit sharing, and bonuses for outstanding work. In addition, the employer usually reimburses all travel expenses. Self-employed consultants have to maintain their own office and provide their own benefits.

Related Occupations.

Management analysts and consultants collect, review, and analyze data, make recommendations, and assist in the implementation of their ideas. Others who use similar skills are managers, computer systems analysts, operations research analysts, economists, and financial analysts. Researchers prepare data and reports for consultants to use in their recommendations.

Sources of Additional Information.

Information about career opportunities in management consulting is available from:

> The Association of Management Consulting Firms
> 521 Fifth Ave., 35th Floor
> New York, NY 10175-3598
>
> Homepage: ***http://www.amcf.org/***

Information on obtaining a management analyst position with the Federal Government may be obtained from the Office of Personnel Management through a telephone-based system. Consult your telephone directory under U.S. Government for a local number or call (912) 757-3000. That number is not toll-free and charges may result. Information also is available from their Internet site: *http:// www.usajobs.opm.gov/*.

Loan Officer

Nature of the Work.

Banks and other financial institutions need up-to-date information on companies and individuals applying for loans and credit. Customers and clients provide this information to the financial institution's loan officers, generally the first employees to be seen by them. Loan officers prepare, analyze, and verify loan applications, make decisions regarding the extension of credit, and help borrowers fill out loan applications. Loan counselors, also called loan collection officers, contact borrowers who have delinquent accounts and help them find a method of repayment to avoid default on the loan.

Commercial and mortgage loan officers behave as sales people who actively seek out potential customers. Commercial loan officers contact firms that may or may not have accounts with their bank. They find out if their potential client is planning any projects for which they may need a loan. If so, loan officers try to establish a relationship with the firm so that the firm will contact them when the loan is needed. Similarly, mortgage loan officers try to develop relationships with commercial or residential real estate agencies. When an individual or firm buys a property, the real estate agent might recommend contacting that loan officer for financing.

Working Conditions.

Commercial and mortgage loan officers frequently work away from their offices, relying on laptop computers, cellular phones, and pagers to keep in contact with their offices and clients. Mortgage loan officers frequently work out of their home or car, often-visiting offices or homes of clients while completing the loan application. Commercial loan officers may travel to other cities to prepare complex loan agreements. Consumer loan officers and loan counselors are likely to spend most of their time in an office.

Most loan officers and counselors work a standard 40-hour week, but may work longer, particularly mortgage loan officers who are free to take on as many customers as they choose. Loan officers usually carry a heavy caseload and sometimes cannot accept new clients until they complete current cases. They are especially busy when interest rates are low, triggering a surge in loan applications.

Employment.

Loan officers and counselors held about 209,000 jobs in 1996. About three out of five are employed by commercial banks, savings institutions, and credit unions. Others are employed by non-bank financial institutions, such as mortgage brokerage firms and personal credit firms. Loan officers are concentrated in urban and suburban areas. In rural areas, the branch or assistant manager often handles the loan application process.

Training, Other Qualifications, and Advancement.

Loan officer positions generally require a bachelor's degree in finance, economics, or a related field. Most employers also prefer applicants who are familiar with computers and their applications in banking. For commercial or mortgage loan officer jobs, training or experience in sales is highly valued by potential employers. A small number of loan officers advance through the ranks in an organization, acquiring several years of work experience in various other occupations, such as teller or customer service representative.

Persons planning a career as a loan officer or counselor should be capable of developing effective working relationships with others, confident in their abilities, and highly motivated. Loan officers must be willing to attend community events as a representative of their employer.

Job Outlook.

While employment in banks—where most loan officers and counselors are found—is projected to decline, employment of loan officers and counselors is expected to grow faster than the average for all occupations through the year 2006. As the population and economy grow, applications for commercial, consumer, and mortgage loans will increase, spurring demand for loan officers and counselors. Growth in the variety and complexity of loans, and the importance of loan officers to the success of banks and other lending institutions, also should assure employment growth. Although increased demand will generate many new jobs, most openings will result from the need to replace workers who leave the occupation or retire. College graduates and those with banking, lending, or sales experience should have the best job prospects.

Loan officers and counselors are less likely to lose their jobs than other workers in banks and other lending institutions during economic downturns. Because loans are the major source of income for banks, loan officers are fundamental to the success of their organizations. Also, many loan officers are compensated in part on a commission basis. Loan counselors are likely to see an increase in the number of delinquent loans during difficult economic times.

Earnings.

The form of compensation for loan officers varies, depending on the lending institution. Some banks offer salary plus commission as an incentive to increase the number of loans processed, while others pay only salaries.

According to a salary survey conducted by Robert Half International, a staffing services firm specializing in accounting and finance, residential real estate mortgage loan officers earned between $30,600 and $45,000 in 1997; commercial real estate mortgage loan officers, between $45,100 and $73,000; consumer loan officers, between $28,900 and $48,000; and commercial lenders, between $37,400 and $85,000. Smaller banks generally paid 15 percent less than larger banks. Loan officers who are paid on a commission basis generally earn more than those on salary only do.

Banks and other lenders sometimes offer their loan officers free checking privileges and somewhat lower interest rates on personal loans.

Related Occupations.

Loan officers help the public manage financial assets and secure loans. Occupations that involve similar functions include securities and financial services sales representatives, financial aid officers, real estate agents and brokers, and insurance agents and brokers.

Sources of Additional Information.

Information about a career as a loan officer or counselor may be obtained from:

American Bankers Association
1120 Connecticut Ave. NW.
Washington, DC 20036

Homepage:
http://www.aba.com/abatool/showme_rel.html?location=homepage

Industrial Production Manager

Nature of the Work.

Industrial production managers coordinate the resources and activities required to produce millions of goods every year in the United States. Although their duties vary from plant to plant, industrial production managers share many of the same major functions. These functions include responsibility for production scheduling, staffing, equipment, quality control, inventory control, and the coordination of production activities with those of other departments.

The primary mission of industrial production managers is planning the production schedule within budgetary limitations and time constraints. This entails analyzing the plant's personnel and capital resources to select the best way of meeting the production quota. Industrial production managers determine which machines will be used, whether overtime or extra shifts are necessary, and the sequence of production. They also monitor the production run to make sure that it stays on schedule and that any problems that may arise are corrected.

Because the work of many departments is interrelated, managers work closely with heads of other departments such as sales, purchasing, and traffic to plan and implement company goals, policies, and procedures. For example, the production manager works with the purchasing department to ensure that plant inventories are maintained at their optimal level.

Working Conditions.

Most industrial production managers divide their time between the shop floor and their offices. While on the floor, they must follow established health and safety practices and wear the required protective clothing and equipment. The time in the office, which is often located on or near the production floor, is usually spent meeting with subordinates or other department managers, analyzing production data, and writing and reviewing reports.

Most industrial production managers work more than 40 hours a week, especially when production deadlines must be met. In facilities that operate around the clock, managers often work late shifts and may be called at any hour to deal with emergencies. This could mean going to the plant to resolve the problem, regardless of the hour, and staying until the situation is under control. Dealing with production workers as well as supervisors when working under the pressure of production deadlines or emergency situations can be stressful. Restructuring that has eliminated levels of management and support staff, shifting more responsibilities to production managers has compounded this stress.

Employment.

Industrial production managers held about 207,000 jobs in 1996. Although employed throughout the manufacturing sector, about one-half are employed in firms that produce industrial machinery and equipment, transportation equipment, electronic and electrical equipment, fabricated metal products, instruments and related products, and food products. Production managers work in all parts of the country, but jobs are most plentiful in areas where manufacturing is concentrated.

Training, Other Qualifications, and Advancement.

Because of the diversity of manufacturing operations and job requirements, there is no standard preparation for this occupation. Many industrial production managers have a college degree in business administration or industrial engineering. Some have a masters degree in business administration (MBA). Others are former production line supervisors who have been promoted.

As production operations become more sophisticated, an increasing number of employers are looking for candidates with MBAs. Companies also are placing greater importance on a candidate's personality. Because the job requires the ability to compromise, persuade, a0nd negotiate, successful production managers must be well rounded and have excellent communication skills.

The few who enter the field directly from college or graduate school often are unfamiliar with the firm's production process. As a result, they may spend their first few months on the job in the company's training program. These programs familiarize trainees with the production line, company policies, and the requirements of the job. In larger companies, these programs may also include assignments to other departments, such as purchasing and accounting. A number of companies hire college graduates as blue-collar worker supervisors and later promote them.

Job Outlook.

Employment of industrial production managers is expected to decline slightly through the year 2006. However, a number of job openings will stem from the need to replace workers who transfer to other occupations or leave the labor force. Applicants with college degrees in business administration or industrial engineering, and particularly those with MBAs and undergraduate engineering degrees, will be in the best position to fill these openings. Employers also are likely to seek candidates who have excellent communication skills, and who are personable, flexible, and eager to participate in ongoing training.

Although manufacturing output is projected to rise, growing productivity among production managers and organizational restructuring will limit the demand for these workers. Productivity gains will result from the widening use of computers for scheduling, planning, and coordination. In addition, just-in-time manufacturing eases scheduling demands, and a growing emphasis on building quality inspection into the production process has redistributed some of the production manager's oversight responsibilities. Because production managers are so integral to the efficient operation of a plant, they have not been greatly affected by recent efforts to flatten management structures. Nevertheless, this trend has led production managers to assume more responsibilities and has discouraged the creation of more employment opportunities.

Earnings.

Salaries of industrial production managers vary significantly by industry and plant size. According to Abbott, Langer, and Associates, the average salary for all production managers was $60,000 in 1996. In addition to salary, industrial production managers may receive bonuses based on job performance.

Related Occupations.

Industrial production managers oversee production staff and equipment, insure that production goals and quality standards are being met, and implement company policies. Individuals with similar functions include materials, operations, purchasing, and traffic managers. Other occupations requiring similar training and skills are sales engineer, manufacturer's sales representative, and industrial engineer.

Sources of Additional Information.

Information on industrial production management can be obtained from:

American Management Association
1601 Broadway
New York, NY 10019.

Homepage: *http://www.amanet.org/usindex.htm*

Human Resource Specialist

Nature of the Work.

Human resources specialists and managers recruit and interview employees, and advise on hiring decisions in accordance with policies and requirements that have been established in conjunction with top management. In an effort to improve morale and productivity and limit job turnover, they also help their firms effectively use employees' skills, provide training opportunities to enhance those skills, and boost employees' satisfaction with their jobs and working conditions. Although some jobs in the human resources field require only limited contact with people outside the office, most involve frequent contact. Dealing with people is an essential part of the job.

Recruiters maintain contacts within the community and may travel extensively, often to college campuses, to search for promising job applicants. Recruiters screen, interview, and test applicants. They may also check references and extend offers of employment to qualified candidates. These workers must be thoroughly familiar with the organization and its personnel policies to discuss wages, working conditions, and promotional opportunities with prospective employees. They must also keep informed about equal employment opportunity (EEO) and affirmative action guidelines and laws, such as the Americans with Disabilities Act.

Employer relations representatives—who usually work in government agencies—maintain working relationships with local employers and promote the use of public employment programs and services. Similarly, employment interviewers—whose many job titles, include personnel consultants, personnel development specialists, and human resources coordinators—help match jobseekers with employers.

Job analysts, sometimes called position classifiers, perform very exacting work. They collect and examine detailed information about job duties to prepare job descriptions. These descriptions explain the duties, training, and skills each job requires. Whenever a large organization introduces a new job or reviews existing jobs, it calls upon the expert knowledge of the job analyst.

Occupational analysts conduct research, generally in large firms. They are concerned with occupational classification systems and study the effects of industry and occupational trends upon worker relationships. They may serve as technical liaison between the firm and industry, government, and labor unions.

Establishing and maintaining a firm's pay system is the principal job of the compensation manager. Assisted by staff specialists, compensation managers devise ways to ensure fair and equitable pay rates. They may conduct surveys to see how their rates compare with others and to see that the firm's pay scale complies with changing laws and regulations. In addition, compensation managers often oversee their firm's performance evaluation system, and they may design reward systems such as pay-for-performance plans.

Employee benefits managers handle the company's employee benefits program, notably its health insurance and pension plans. Expertise in designing and administering benefits programs continues to gain importance as employer-provided benefits account for a growing proportion of overall compensation costs, and as benefit plans increase in number and complexity.

Employee assistance plan managers—also called employee welfare managers—are responsible for a wide array of programs covering occupational safety and health standards and practices, health promotion and physical fitness, medical examinations, and minor health treatment, such as first aid, plant security; publications, food service and recreation activities, car pooling, employee suggestion systems, child care and elder care, and counseling services.

Training and development managers supervise training. Increasingly, management recognizes that training offers a way of developing skills, enhancing productivity and quality of work, and building loyalty to the firm. Training is widely accepted as a method of improving employee morale, but this is only one of the reasons for its growing importance.

Working Conditions.

Personnel work generally takes place in clean, pleasant, and comfortable office settings. Arbitrators and mediators may work out of their homes. Many human resources specialists and managers work a standard 35- to 40-hour week. However, longer hours might be necessary for some workers—for example, labor relations specialists and managers, arbitrators, and mediators—when contract agreements are being prepared and negotiated.

Although most human resources specialists and managers work in the office, some travel extensively. For example, recruiters regularly attend professional meetings and visit college campuses to interview prospective employees. Arbitrators and mediators often must travel to the site chosen for negotiations.

<u>Employment.</u>

Human resources specialists and managers held about 544,000 jobs in 1996. They were employed in virtually every industry. Specialists accounted for three out of five positions; managers, two out of five. About 15,000 specialists were self-employed, working as consultants to public and private employers.

The private sector accounted for about 86 percent of salaried jobs. Among these salaried jobs, services industries—including business, health, social, management, and educational services—accounted for four out of ten jobs; labor organizations, the largest employer among specific industries, accounted for one out of ten. Manufacturing industries accounted for two out of ten jobs, while finance, insurance, and real estate firms accounted for about one out of ten.

Federal, State and local governments employed about 14 percent of salaried human resources specialists and managers. They handled the recruitment, interviewing, job classification, training, salary administration, benefits, employee relations, and related matters of the nation's public employees.

<u>Training, Other Qualifications, and Advancement.</u>

Because of the diversity of duties and level of responsibility, the educational backgrounds of human resources specialists and managers vary considerably. In filling entry-level jobs, employers generally seek college graduates. Some employers prefer applicants who have majored in human resources, personnel administration, or industrial and labor relations; others look for college graduates with a technical or business background; and still others feel that a well-rounded liberal arts education is best.

Many colleges and universities have programs leading to a degree in personnel, human resources, or labor relations. Some offer degree programs in personnel administration or human resources management, training and development, or compensation and benefits. Depending on the school, courses leading to a career in human resources management may be found in departments of business administration, education, instructional technology, organizational development, human services, communication, or public administration, or within a separate human resources institution or department.

The human resources field demands a range of personal qualities and skills. Human resources specialists and managers must speak and write effectively, work with or supervise people having various cultural backgrounds, levels of education, and experience, cope with conflicting points of view, and the unexpected and unusual, function under pressure, and demonstrate integrity, fair-mindedness, and a persuasive, congenial personality.

Entry-level workers often enter formal or on-the-job training programs in which they learn how to classify jobs, interview applicants, or administer employee benefits. They then are assigned to specific areas in the personnel department to gain experience. Later, they may advance to a managerial position, overseeing a major element of the personnel program—compensation or training, for example.

Job Outlook.

The job market for human resources specialists and managers is likely to remain competitive through 2006. This is due to an abundant supply of qualified college graduates and experienced workers. It is true in spite of large numbers of annual job openings that will stem from the need to replace workers who transfer to other jobs, retire, or stop working for other reasons coupled with projected average employment growth.

New jobs will stem from increasing efforts throughout industry to recruit and retain quality employees. Employers are expected to devote greater resources to job-specific training programs in response to the increasing complexity of many jobs, the aging of the work force, and technological advances that can leave employees with obsolete skills. In addition, legislation and court rulings setting standards in occupational safety and health, equal employment opportunity, wages, and health, pension, family leave, and other benefits, will increase demand for experts in these areas. Rising health care costs, in particular, should spur demand for specialists to develop creative compensation and benefits packages that firms can offer prospective employees.

Employment of labor relations staff, including arbitrators and mediators, should grow as firms become more involved in labor relations, and attempt to resolve potentially costly labor-management disputes out of court. Additional job growth may stem from increasing demand for specialists in international human resources management and human resources information systems.

Employment demand should be strong among firms involved in management, consulting, and personnel supply, as businesses increasingly contract out personnel functions or hire personnel specialists on a temporary basis to meet the increasing cost and complexity of training and development programs. Demand should also increase in firms that develop and administer complex employee benefits and compensation packages for other organizations.

Job growth could be limited by the widespread use of computerized human resources information systems that make workers more productive. Similar to other workers, employment of human resources specialists and managers, particularly in larger firms, may be adversely affected by corporate downsizing and restructuring.

Earnings

According to a salary survey conducted by the National Association of Colleges and Employers, bachelor's degree candidates majoring in human resources, including labor relations, received starting offers averaging $25,300 a year in 1996; master's degree candidates, $39,900.

According to a 1996 survey of compensation in the human resources field, conducted by Abbott, Langer, and Associates of Crete, Illinois, the median total cash compensation for selected personnel and labor relations occupations were:

Industrial/labor relations directors	$106,100
Divisional human resources directors	91,300
Compensation and benefits directors	90,500
Employee/community relations directors	87,500
Training and organizational directors	86,600
Benefits directors	80,500
Plant/location human resources managers	64,400
Recruitment and interviewing managers	63,800
Compensation supervisors	53,400
Training generalists	49,900
Employment interviewing supervisors	42,800
Safety specialists	42,500

Job evaluation specialists	39,600
Employee assistance/employee counseling specialists	39,000
Human resources information systems specialists	38,800
Benefits specialists	38,300
E.E.O./affirmative action specialists	38,200
Training material development specialists	37,200
Employee services/employee recreation specialists	35,000

According to a survey of workplaces in 160 metropolitan areas, personnel specialists with limited experience had median earnings of $25,700 a year in 1995, the middle-half earned between $23,700 and $28,500 a year. Personnel supervisors/managers with limited experience had median earnings of $59,000 a year. The middle-half earned between $54,000 and $65,200 a year.

In the Federal Government in 1997, persons with a bachelor degree or three years general experience in the personnel field generally started at $19,500 a year. Those with a superior academic record or an additional year of specialized experience started at $24,200 a year. Those with a master's degree may start at $29,600, and those with a doctorate in a personnel field may start at $35,800. Beginning salaries were slightly higher in areas where the prevailing local pay level was higher.

Personnel specialists in the Federal Government averaged $52,900 a year in 1997; personnel managers, $55,400.

Related Occupations.

All human resources occupations are closely related. Other workers with skills and expertise in interpersonal relations include employment, rehabilitation, and college career planning and placement counselors, lawyers, psychologists, sociologists, social workers, public relations specialists, and teachers.

Sources of Additional Information.

For information about careers in employee training and development, contact:

American Society for Training and Development
1640 King St., Box 1443
Alexandria, VA 22313

Homepage: *http://www.dc.astd.org/*

For information about careers and certification in employee compensation and benefits, contact:

American Compensation Association
14040 Northsight Blvd.
Scottsdale, AZ 85260
Homepage: *http://www.acaonline.org/*

For information about careers in arbitration and other aspects of dispute resolution, contact:

American Arbitration Association
140 West 51st St.
New York, NY 10020
Phone: (800) 778-7879
Homepage: *http://www.adr.org/*

5.11 The Labor Force and Industry Employment Growth

You will need to consider a number of factors as you make your decision to chose a major and then eventually an industry in which you would like to work. The projected growth of the labor force and the projected growth of industry employment should be given consideration as you establish your goals for the future. The Bureau of Labor Statistics (BLS) releases projections on the labor force and the ten industries with the fastest employment growth [8]. Using the information from the previous section to select your major and then matching your major choice to an employment growth industry will improve your chances to be selected for an internship and subsequent employment.

Labor Force

The labor force is projected to increase by 15 million over the 1996-2006 period, from 134 million to 149 million. This represents an increase of 11 percent. The projections indicate that the demographic composition of the labor force is expected to change because the population itself will change and because work force participation will change.

The labor force in the age group 45-64 will grow faster than the labor force of any other age group as the baby-boom generation (born 1946-64) continues to age. The labor force 25 to 34 years of age is projected to decline by almost 3 million, reflecting the decrease in births in the late 1960s and early 1970s.

Industry employment

Over the 1996-2006 period, total employment is projected to increase by 14 percent or 19 million, from 132 million in 1996 to 151 million in 2006. This growth rate is much slower than during the previous 10-year period 1986-1996 when growth was 19 percent and the economy gained 21 million additional jobs.

Service-producing industries will account for virtually all of the job growth. Only construction will add jobs in the goods-producing sector, offsetting declines in manufacturing and mining. Health services, business services, social services, and engineering, management, and related services are expected to account for almost one of every two wage and salary worker jobs added to the economy during the 1996-2006 period. Of the ten fastest growing industries, nine belong to one of these four industry groups. The ten occupations adding the most jobs will account for more than one-fifth of total employment growth.

Ten Industries with the Fastest Projected Employment Growth 1996–2006

Industry	Employment		Change	
	1996	2006	#	%
Computer and data processing	1,208	2,509	1,301	108
Health services	1,172	1,968	796	68
Management and public relations	873	1,400	527	60
Transportation services	204	327	123	60
Residential care	672	1,070	398	59
Personnel supply services	2,646	4,039	1,393	53
Water and sanitation	231	349	118	51
Miscellaneous social services	846	1,266	420	50
Offices of health practitioners	2,751	4,046	1,295	47
Amusement and recreation	1,109	1,565	457	41

[NOTE: Employment numbers in thousands]

Table available at:

http://www.stats.bls.gov/news.release/ecopro.table4.htm

Summary

In this chapter you were introduced to business as a profession. You were encouraged to take every opportunity to learn about business. This will be a lifelong process, but it should begin now.

Ten of the most important rewards and opportunities that will be yours if you are successful in graduating in business were presented and discussed. It is important to have a clear picture of what all the hard work and personal sacrifice will mean to the quality of your life.

We next assisted you in developing an articulate answer to a question you are likely to be asked frequently: "What can you do with a business education?" You learned that business is the process of developing a product or process to meet a customer need or perceived opportunity. You also learned that business professionals can be categorized both by their academic discipline and by their job function. And we explored many of those disciplines and some of the most common job functions. You also learned about some of the employment opportunities that will exist for you upon graduation.

Finally, you were informed of the ten industries which are projected to have the largest employment growth. You may want to consider preparing yourself for employment in one of these "hot" industries.

References

1. *The American Heritage Dictionary of the English Language*, Houghton Mifflin Company, Boston, 1976

2. Jacobs, Joseph J., *The Anatomy of an Entrepreneur*, ICS Press, Institute for Contemporary Studies, San Francisco, California, 1991.

3. Iacocca, Lee, *Iacocca, An Autobiography*, Bantam Books, New York, 1984.

4. Armstrong, Neil, *First on the Moon. A Voyage with Neil Armstrong*, Little Town, Boston, 1970.

5. U.S. Department of Education, National Center For Education Statistics, Higher Formal Awards Conferred Surveys, and Integrated

Postsecondary Education Data System, Table 250 (table prepared July 1997), Washington DC.

6. Lumsdaine, Edward and Lumsdaine, Monika, *Creative Problem Solving*: *Thinking Skills for a Changing World,* 2nd Edition, McGraw-Hill, New York, 1993.

7. "$alary $urvey: A Study of 1995-1996 Beginning Offers," National Association of Colleges and Employers, 62 Highland Avenue, Bethlehem, PA 18017, September 1996.

8. "1998-99 Occupational Outlook Handbook" Bureau of Labor Statistics, Bureau of Labor Statistics, Publications Sales Center, P.O. Box 2145, Chicago, IL 60690 (WEB Site:
    http://stats.bls.gov/oco/oco1000.htm)

Exercises

1. Write a one-page paper outlining the influences (teachers, parents, TV, etc.) that led you to choose business as your major.

2. Develop a list of activities you can engage in that will increase your understanding of business careers. Develop a plan for implementing some of these activities.

3. Add ten or more additional items to the list of rewards and opportunities of a business career presented in Section 5.2. Pick your top ten from the total list and rank them in order of importance.

4. Have you ever had a job you didn't like? Describe the job. What didn't you like about it?

5. Pick one of the business disciplines listed in Section 5.3. Write a 500-word paper describing that discipline.

6. As indicated in Section 5.2, business graduates make up approximately 21 percent of all college graduates. Go to your career planning and placement office and find out how many employers interview on campus annually. What percentage of those employers interview business graduates?

7. Which of the business disciplines listed in Section 5.3 are offered by your business college? Are there other disciplines offered? How many students graduate annually in each of these disciplines?

8. Which of the business job functions presented in Section 5.4 through 5.10 is the most appealing to you? Write a one-page paper describing why.

9. Interview a business professional. Find out the following: (1) What business discipline did he or she study? (2) What business discipline does he or she use in the current job? (3) What industry sector does he or she work in? (4) What percentage of his or her time is spent in the various basic business functions (planning, staffing, leading, controlling, etc.)?

10. Develop a list of attributes that would be desirable for one of the business job functions described in Section 5.4 through 5.10.

11. Make a list of the responsibilities and obligations you will incur when you become a business professional.

Chapter 6
ORIENTATION TO THE
BUSINESS EDUCATION SYSTEM

Introduction

If you are to take full advantage of your business education opportunities, the first thing you must know is how the educational system works. And the added bonus is as you better understand the education system and make that system work for you, you will develop your ability to understand other systems you will encounter in the future. Through this process you will gain the skills needed to make those systems work for you as well.

First we will first give an overview of **how business education is organized** and how the business programs are organized within the university. Then we will provide you with an overview of the business education system by looking at the criteria the **AACSB (The International Association for Management Education)** requires all accredited business programs to meet. Understanding the criteria can provide you with insight into the key elements of your business program: mission, faculty, curriculum, instructional resources, students, and intellectual contributions.

Next, we will examine important **academic regulations, policies, and procedures** in three areas: 1) academic performance; 2) enrollment; and 3) student rights. Only by understanding these regulations, policies, and procedures at your institution will you be able to make optimal use of the educational system.

Finally, we will consider opportunities for education beyond the bachelor's degree level. The benefits of pursuing **the MBA and/or Ph.D. degrees in business** will be discussed. Among those benefits are the advanced knowledge gained through the additional course work and the research skills gained by working on a thesis or dissertation under the close supervision of a faculty adviser. We will describe opportunities to pursue **post-graduate study in disciplines other than business.**

6.1 Organization of Business Education

A business department (e.g., Department of Accounting, Department of Economics) administers each of the business programs at a university. A department generally administers only one business program but in some cases a single department (e.g., Department of Accounting and Finance) administers two or three programs. A department chair or department head heads each department.

Generally, all of the business departments at a university are organized into a school of business or a college of business. A dean of business heads the school or college.

The business college is only one of several colleges or schools on a university campus. Other colleges/schools may include the College of Engineering, the College of Arts and Letters, the College of Science, and the School of Architecture. All of the schools or colleges on a campus are organized into the academic affairs unit headed by a *Provost or Vice President for Academic Affairs* or a *Vice Chancellor for Academic Affairs*.

The Provost or Vice President for Academic Affairs or Vice Chancellor for Academic Affairs reports to the *President* or *Chancellor* of the university. The president or chancellor oversees the entire university. The primary areas that form the university organization in addition to academic affairs are fiscal management, facilities management, information resources management, student affairs, institutional advancement, and auxiliary services.

The typical administrative organization of the university from a business department chair to the president is shown at the top of the next page.

6.2 Business Education Accreditation

The **AACSB (The International Association for Management Education)** is the premier accreditation body for bachelors, masters and doctoral degree programs in business administration and accounting. The AACSB is a not-for-profit corporation of educational institutions, corporations and other organizations devoted to the promotion and improvement of higher education in business administration and management [1]. The AACSB was formerly known as the American Association of Collegiate Systems for Business. The new name was adopted July 1, 1997 to reflect the changing world of business. "AACSB"

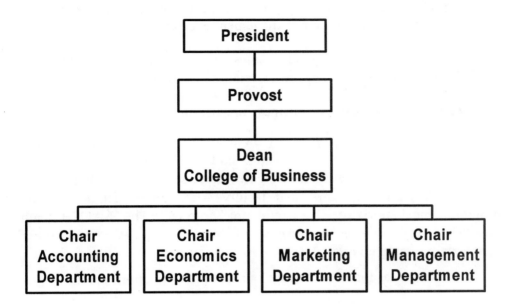

was kept as the acronym for the organization because of its name recognition.

The AACSB membership consists of over 650 U.S. educational institutions, over 100 international educational associations and approximately 70 business, government, and nonprofit institutions. AACSB institutions annually grant over 85 percent of all degrees awarded in business and management education in the United States. AACSB is also the professional organization for management education.

In addition to its accreditation function, AACSB conducts:

- an extensive array of development programs for faculty and administrators

- engages in research and survey projects on topics specific to the field of management education

- represents U.S. business schools with respect to federal policies and funding legislation

- maintains relationships with disciplinary associations and other groups

- interacts with the corporate community on a variety of projects and initiatives

- produces a wide variety of publications and special reports on trends and issues within management education. [1]

A good way to understand business education is to understand the accreditation process. Each of the association members is evaluated by the AACSB approximately every ten years. A peer review team representing the AACSB evaluates all aspects of the business program.

Prior to the visit, the peer review team members receive *self-study accreditation reports* from the business college (the accounting program may be accredited separately if elected). These self-studies—prepared by the dean, department chairs, and faculty—describe in detail how the programs meet and exceed accreditation criteria. The AACSB team members also receive transcripts of recent graduates and other supplemental material related to each business program.

Primary areas that are evaluated against AACSB criteria are:

Mission Determination
Faculty Development
Curriculum Planning
Instructional Delivery
Student Selection and Service
Intellectual Contributions

The objective of the accreditation process is to assist business and accounting programs in preparing students to contribute to their organizations and to society, and to grow personally and professionally throughout their careers. Programs that meet the criteria are accredited for a ten-year period. Programs with minor deficiencies will either be revisited in three years or required to write a report at the three-year point to document progress in correcting the deficiencies. Serious deficiencies can result in the program being put on probation, which could lead to eventual loss of accreditation.

The following sections discuss the important areas of mission, faculty, curriculum, instruction, students, and intellectual contributions as they generally relate to undergraduate accreditation. The descriptions are adapted from the AACSB Accreditation Handbook [2]. As you progress through your business program, you may want to do your own evaluation as to how your program measures up against these standards.

Mission Determination

The business school should articulate its mission as a guide to its view of the future, its planned evolution, and its infrastructure and use of resources. The school's mission statement must be clear and published, appropriate to higher education, specify the educational objectives of each degree program offered, and specify the relative emphasis on teaching, intellectual contributions, and service. The mission statement serves as the basis of the accreditation process. I would encourage you to ask for and review a copy of your business school's mission statement.

To meet the AACSB standard a school must demonstrate that its mission:

- Emphasizes the achievement of high quality in each of its degree programs

- Is the outcome of a process in which the viewpoints of various constituencies have been considered

- Is reviewed periodically and revised as needed

- Is consistent with instructional resources

Faculty Development

According to the AACSB:

> *The heart of any educational program is the faculty. The faculty's composition and qualifications are essential to the school's educational programs. These qualifications are key to creating and delivering high quality degree programs.*

Each business school recruits, develops and maintains a faculty to accomplish its mission with respect to instruction, intellectual contribution and service. A variety of faculty skills are needed to meet any school's mission. Faculty resources and faculty management should be consistent with the school's mission statement. The faculty composition and qualifications are judged by the following factors:

- *Faculty Management Resource Plan which establishes faculty size, composition, qualifications and development. This process must consider the school's teaching, intellectual contributions and professional service responsibilities.*

- *Faculty Recruitment, Selection and Orientation Plan which should be consistent with the school's mission and demonstrate continuous efforts to achieve demographic diversity.*

- *Faculty Development, Promotion, Retention and Renewal should reflect the school's mission and the demanding competitive and technological challenges faced by business. Processes should be in place to determine appropriate teaching loads; formal periodic reviews for reappointment, promotion and tenure decisions; and continuing faculty intellectual development and renewal including support for faculty participation in academic and professional organizations.*

- *Faculty Size, Composition, and Deployment Plan should maintain a full-time faculty sufficient to provide stability and ongoing improvement for the degree programs offered.*

- *Faculty, in aggregate, should have sufficient academic and professional qualifications to accomplish the school's mission. Academic qualification requires a combination of original academic preparation (degree completion) augmented by subsequent activities that maintain or establish preparation for current teaching responsibilities.*

Curriculum Planning

Curricula (i.e., the specific coursework required by each program) are central to the implementation of a degree program. Creating and delivering high quality curricula requires planning and evaluation. Undergraduate curricula provide a broad context within which education for business is set. These curricula combine general education and basic study of business. To meet the standard:

- Undergraduate curriculum content should provide an understanding of perspectives that form the context for business. Coverage should include:

  -Ethical and global issues

  -The influence of political, social, legal and regulatory, environmental and technological issues

  -The impact of demographic diversity on an organization

- Undergraduate curriculum should have a general education component that normally comprises 50 percent of a four-year program.

- Undergraduate curriculum should include foundation knowledge for business in the following areas:

  -Accounting

  -Behavioral science

  -Economics

  -Mathematics and Statistics

  -Written and Oral Communications

- Business schools should require a minimum of 50 percent of business credit hours be earned at the degree-awarding institution.

- Curriculum for each degree program should be the result of a curriculum planning process and should be consistent with the business school's mission.

- Each degree program should be systematically monitored to assess its effectiveness and should be revised to reflect new objectives and to incorporate improvements based on contemporary theory and practice.

Instructional Delivery

The instructional program is the central activity of a business school and must be effective. This effectiveness is influenced by the availability of resources and by the way the instructional program is managed, delivered, and evaluated. The school's faculty must assume the primary responsibility for the relevance of what is taught and the means by which it is delivered to the students. To meet the standard:

- Instructional resources must be available to meet the instructional objectives of the programs offered.

- Instructional technologies and related support should be available and utilized by the faculty

- Students must have access to and be *required* to make use of library and computing facilities

- Space, facilities and staff support should be adequate to meet program goals and objectives

- Faculty are responsible for effectiveness, creation and delivery of instruction

- Faculty are responsible for the evaluation of instructional effectiveness and student achievement

- Faculty are responsible for the continued improvement of instructional programs

- Faculty are responsible for innovation in the instructional process

- Individual faculty are responsible for currency in their instructional fields

- Individual faculty are responsible for delivery of effective instruction

- Individual faculty are responsible for their accessibility to students

Student Selection and Service

A direct link exists between a school's mission and the characteristics of the students served by the educational programs. Student selection and program design are an interdependent process. Careful planning and execution of these processes are essential to quality education.

To meet the AACSB student standard:

- Student selection must be consistent with the school's mission.

- The student selection process should demonstrate continuous efforts to achieve demographic diversity in student enrollment.

- Admission and retention policies should be clear and consistent with the objective of producing high quality graduates.

- There should be clear identification of a systematic plan of student services available for advisement and placement.

Intellectual Contributions

Producing intellectual contributions represents a core set of responsibilities of higher education for business. Such contributions improve management theory and practice and support the present and future quality of instruction. The intellectual contributions have been grouped as follows: basic scholarship, applied scholarship, and instructional development. The school's mission influences the relative emphasis among the types of intellectual contribution. However, all schools should have some of their intellectual contributions committed to instructional development.

To meet the AACSB intellectual standards:

- Intellectual contributions should be available for scrutiny by academic peers or practitioners. The components of intellectual contributions to be judged are as follows.

  - Basic Scholarship. The creation of new knowledge

  - Applied Scholarship. The application, transfer and interpretation of knowledge to improve management practice and teaching

  - Instructional Development. The enhancement of educational value of instructional efforts of the institution or discipline.

AACSB The New Criteria

You should be aware that AACSB is continually evaluating and updating the accreditation criteria. The new criteria, as it is developed, will be phased in with current accreditation visits. For the most part your institution's business program was developed in response to the accreditation criteria described in the previous sections. However, in the next few years, you may observe many changes as your institution responds to the new criteria. You can find more information on AACSB Accreditation on the AACSB's website:

http://www.aacsb.edu/opt1.html

6.3 Academic Advising

As previously stated by AACSB:

> *The business program must assume the responsibility of assuring that the students receive proper curricular and career advising.*

Academic advising, including both curricular advising and career advising, is extremely important. I hope you are studying in a business college in which the faculty take academic advising seriously.

On the other hand, you may not be getting the quality and quantity of academic advising you need. Unfortunately, sometimes the demands of teaching and research result in a less than satisfactory student advising process. I have participated in and analyzed numerous student surveys and one point appears to be universal:

> *Probably the most neglected area in education is advising, and certainly this is the area where students show the least satisfaction.*

This statement has been borne out by my personal experience as follows.

A Personal Anecdote

> *"How is your advising system?" The university administrator usually states something like this. "We have a great advising system. Each student is assigned a faculty or staff adviser with whom he or she meets each term to plan their course program for the next term. The adviser reviews past performance, works out the student's course program for the next term, and gives the student some career guidance." Then I ask students "How does the advising system work here?" More often than not students will tell me: "I leave my advising form with the department secretary to get my adviser's signature and I pick it up the next day."*

Quality and Quantity

The absence of academic advising is not the only problem. An equally serious problem is bad advising.

You may find academic advisers who give you bad advice. One common area of bad advice comes from faculty who feel that you should take a "full load" every term in order to graduate "on time" or you haven't measured up. They will almost insist that you take 16-18 units whether this is best for you or not. These advisors don't account for the fact that you have a particularly demanding schedule of courses or that you may be working twenty hours a week or that you would be willing to go to summer school to "keep up."

Bad advice can also occur when advisers don't have accurate and up-to-date information about the curriculum or about various rules and regulations that affect your academic status. I have a constant stream of students telling me things like the following. "My adviser told me I could try out this course and drop it later." "My adviser told me it would be okay to take 20 units." "My adviser told me that ACCT 322 has been eliminated from the curriculum." The worst scenario is when "my advisor" turns out to be another student who has good intentions but creates disastrous results for you! Sometimes I can remedy the situation; other times I can't. Remember: **Ignorance is no excuse!**

Take Personal Responsibility for Getting Proper Advising

My recommendation is that you take personal responsibility for getting proper academic advising. After all, who suffers when you fail to be advised or get bad advice? You do! There are several possible sources for academic advising including professors, advising staff, or other students. But do not rely solely on word of mouth. **Know the rules.**

The first step is to make sure you understand how the advising system is structured at your institution. There are large differences in how business programs handle advising. At some institutions, advising is mandatory; whereas, at others it is optional. One department may assign each student an individual faculty adviser; another department may have a principal faculty adviser who advises all first year students. Some schools have advising centers with professional staff who do the advising. Whatever, the advising system at your institution, I encourage you to take full advantage of it.

If you are assigned an academic adviser, whether a faculty member or professional staff member, I strongly recommend you schedule a meeting PRIOR TO THE COURSE REGISTRATION PERIOD with your adviser to plan your courses, whether such a meeting is mandatory or optional. If you have not been assigned an advisor, do not wait for the system to assign someone. Ask your department chair or the assistant dean or the dean for an adviser. An advising session will provide you the opportunity to gain feedback on your academic performance to date, ask any questions you might have about academic policies or regulations, work out your course program for the next term, and discuss your overall career objectives.

Fellow students can be good sources of supplemental information as well. Other students can be particularly helpful in identifying the best teachers. One warning: Be sure to find out the reason a student identifies a professor as "the best." Professors are not just *good* or *bad*, they are also *hard* or *easy*. Sometimes when a students says that Professor "X" is good, they really mean that Professor "X" is easy. I hope you will seek out professors who are good teachers but set high standards of performance.

Any advice you get should be tempered with your own judgment. Using your institution's catalog and schedule of classes, you can figure out a great deal. Your university or college may publish a *Student Handbook*. These publications contain an enormous amount of information. But you won't get that information unless you read them.

For example, your entire curriculum is laid out in your university catalog. I would encourage you to develop a plan for what courses you will take each term throughout your undergraduate study. Have your academic adviser review your plan and then start following it. You can always change your plan as needed in the future.

6.4 Academic Regulations

It is also essential that you to work toward understanding important academic regulations, policies, and procedures. Not knowing about some of these can hurt you; knowing about others can help you. Your university catalog or policies handbook contains much of this information. There are also regulations, policies, and procedures that are specific to an academic unit which may or may not be in the university catalog. Your college or department may publish a *Student Handbook* that can be an even better source of information for you.

One Last Story

> *I have always been a person who tried to understand the way systems worked and how to best make those systems work for me. When I started my current position, I assumed that university students would be very concerned with the policies of the institution, since the policies outlined the path for academic success. You can imagine my surprise when I asked the first ten students I advised whether they had read the student handbook and the common answer was "I saw that book when I moved into my dorm, but I never read it. I figured someone would tell me what I needed to know."*
>
> *Unfortunately for all ten of these students they were asking for "exemption" from one school policy or another due to the fact they had not been aware of the rules. Each of the students learned a very valuable lesson. "<u>Ignorance of the rules is not an excuse.</u>" I could have offered alternatives if only the students had read the handbook and talked to me prior to the start of the semester, rather than coming to me afterwards seeking an exemption.*

I hope my brief story has embedded in you the importance of understanding the academic regulations and procedures of your college and university. Doing so can ensure your academic success and even allow you to experience some unexpected academic opportunities.

Let me give you a few examples. Do you know the upper limit on the number of units you can take in any one semester? Do you know whether you can do an independent study project with your favorite professor and substitute it for a required course? Can you take courses at another institution during the summer and transfer them back to your university? Can you structure your curriculum to enhance your chances of getting a job or your chances of acceptance into graduate school?

The following sections give brief overviews of important regulations, policies, and procedures that you should find out about. These are divided into three categories:

1) academic performance

2) enrollment policies

3) student rights.

Academic Performance

Your success as a student will be measured in large part by your *grade point average* (*GPA*). I can assure you from personal experience that grades **are** important. When I interviewed for my current position, I was asked to submit transcripts of all my college work, and I had completed my undergraduate work 11 years before! When you interview for your first job, you *might* be asked to submit transcripts, but certainly *will* be asked about your grade point average. Unlike other factors which are qualitative and difficult to evaluate, your grade point average is quantitative and therefore is likely to get more emphasis than it really deserves. If your grade point average is below a certain level, some employers will eliminate you from consideration solely on that basis. Whether this practice is proper or fair is irrelevant; it is a reality you have to face.

There are a number of regulations, policies, and procedures which impact your overall academic performance. First and foremost is the way your grade point average is calculated, but others such as the opportunity to take courses pass/fail, incompletes, repeat grade policy, academic renewal, and credit by examination can impact your opportunity to build a strong grade point average.

Grade Point Average. Most universities operate on a 4.0 grade point system as follows:

Grade Symbol	Explanation	Grade Points/Unit
A	Outstanding	4
B	Very Good	3
C	Average	2
D	Barely Passing	1
F	Failure	0

Many universities give pluses and minuses. This certainly makes it easier for faculty to grade. Deciding between an *A* and a *B* or a *B* and a *C* grade in borderline cases can be a difficult decision for faculty. Having *A-* and *B+* or *B-* and *C+* as options makes assigning grades a lot easier.

Your total *grade points* for a term are computed by adding up the product of the credit hours for each course times the grade points corresponding to the letter grade you receive for that course. Your *grade point average* is computed by dividing the total grade points by the total number of credit hours taken.

One last point about your GPA. It's very important that you get off to a good start. Once you have several years behind you, it's very difficult to pull up your GPA. But the converse is true as well. If you establish a good GPA early on, it's difficult to pull it down.

Pass/Fail or Credit/No Credit. Many universities offer students the opportunity to take some courses on a Pass/Fail (P/F) basis or Credit/No Credit (CR/NC) basis. Courses taken in this manner normally do not affect your grade point average. Generally, major requirements cannot be taken via this method and the total number of units that can be taken on this basis is limited. The benefit of this option, if available, is that it allows you to take courses outside of your areas of strength without the risk of lowering your GPA. Some universities do count a failed P/F course in your GPA. Check out the rules thoroughly!

Add/Drop. All universities have a last date to add or to drop a course. The last add date allows you to make a change to your class schedule a few days into the term. The exact number of days is determined by each university, usually you will have about one week to make the adjustments to your schedule. The last date to drop a course is normally much later into the term than the last add date. Some universities allow you to drop a course and your academic record will not record the fact you attempted the course. Others assign a grade of "W" to indicate a drop from the course and still others assign a grade of "WP" or "WF" indicating passing or failing at the time of the drop.

Incomplete. When you are unable to complete a course for justifiable reason (illness, family crisis), you probably can request a grade of *incomplete (I)* from your professor. Generally, the incomplete must be made up within a certain time period. The additional time can, however, provide you the opportunity to achieve a higher level of mastery in the course than if you tried to deal with it in the midst of a personal crisis.

Repeat Grade Policy. Some universities allow you, under specific conditions, to repeat a course and count only the higher of the two grades you receive in your grade point average. Generally, you are only allowed to take advantage of this regulation for a limited number of courses. Some universities only allow you to repeat courses in which you have received a grade of *D* or *F*. But at some universities, you can even repeat a course to raise a grade of *C* to a *B* or a *B* to an *A*. Check your campus regulations on this.

Academic Renewal. Your university may have a policy that allows students to apply to remove one or more entire terms of previous work from their academic record. Generally, this can only be done under very restrictive circumstances. This policy is designed to provide forgiveness to students who had one or two terms in which their academic performance was extremely low, *and* there are justifiable circumstances why the performance was not representative.

Credit by Exam. Most universities permit students to challenge some courses by examination. This may not be a "free ride" because whatever grade is received on the examination, including a grade of *F,* is generally averaged into your grade point average. Other universities may award credit hours but not grades for successful credit by examination.

Probation. If your grades fall below a certain level, you will be placed on probation. Being placed on probation is a serious warning and indicates that unless your academic performance improves, you will be dismissed. Some universities require that students who go on probation receive mandatory academic counseling and/or reduce the number of units they take. Most universities have very stringent rules concerning both consecutive terms on probation and the number of probation terms allowed.

Dismissal. Continued poor academic performance will lead to dismissal. "Flunking out" is no fun and should be avoided at all cost. Policies for reinstatement following dismissal vary significantly from one institution to the next. Some institutions will reinstate students immediately following a first dismissal; others require students to drop out of school for a period of time. Disqualified students may be required to earn their way back by taking courses at another institution and achieving a predetermined grade point average. If you are dismissed a second or third time, you could be permanently barred from attending the university.

Dean's List. On the opposite end of the spectrum is the *Dean's List*. This is a very prestigious honor that is awarded each term to students who achieve a certain level of excellence. Check your university's requirements, but *Dean's List* status generally goes to full-time students whose grades are above a set level or are in the top five percent of students in their major.

Graduation Requirements. Universities normally require that in order to graduate you must have at least a 2.0 ("C") grade point average in all courses attempted. You may also be required to achieve at least a 2.0 grade point average in your major. Other categories of courses such as all courses in general education or university requirements may have a specific GPA requirement. Some other typical graduation requirements could include a time limit on courses taken and evidence of skills acquisition such as, for example, passing a writing proficiency exam.

Graduation with Honors. One of the greatest recognitions you can receive, as a student, is to graduate with honors. There are generally three levels of honors: 1) Cum laude (top 5%); 2) Magna cum laude (top 3%); and 3) Summa cum laude (top 1%). Some universities use specific overall GPAs in lieu of percentages for the award of honors at graduation. Receipt of these prestigious honors is usually designated on the diploma and on the permanent transcript.

Enrollment and Registration

Every university has a number of regulations, policies, and procedures related to enrollment and registration. These range from how you notify the university that you intend to enroll to how you go about selecting or changing your major to how you select your classes. A number of the most important of these procedures are outlined below.

Selecting Your College and Major. The procedure by which students select their college and major varies from one institution to the next. Some places require students to designate a specific college and major as part of their initial application process. At others, students are admitted as college "intents" or "undecided" and must apply after their first or second year for admission into a specific college and/or major based on their academic performance.

Selecting a specific major or discipline can be difficult. Your selection should be based on factors including your aptitude, your interest, your graduate school intentions, and employment opportunities—factors about which you may have limited information. At some universities there is a common core of courses required by all disciplines and your decision can be postponed until the sophomore, junior, or even senior year. For programs that have a highly specialized curriculum requiring an early decision, you may be forced into a decision before you have adequate information.

My advice is to keep your options open as long as your curriculum will permit. As you progress through the curriculum, you will be in a better position to choose because you will gain insights and information from your advisers, professors, your course work, your pre-professional employment experiences, your peers, and from business professionals.

Changing Your Major. Don't feel that you must stay with your initial choice of major. As indicated in the previous section, you will gain insights along the way that will enable you to make a more informed decision about your "life's work." I started out as a civil engineering major since my father informed me it was a good choice. I didn't like my early surveying courses nor did I care for Physics II and changed to business administration. I started out assuming I would be an accounting major but eventually ended up as a management major after about two years of college experience.

My philosophy is summarized by the thought that:

> *Early decisions about majors are normally based on well-intentioned advice and emotion. The final decision on your major should be based on academic advising, academic work, pre-professional work experience, and personal preference.*

Don't be worried if you're not sure about your end objective. View your college years as a chance to explore with the goal of finding what you like. Take advantage of the opportunities afforded to you. There are no bad experiences, but rather every experience helps you to define your path to success.

One warning: You will need to explore the procedures for changing your major from one discipline to another. Changing majors is sometimes very easy and sometimes very difficult. Do not assume that you will be able to change into whatever major you desire.

Double Majors/Minors. You can choose to have more than one major or to have a minor. Students with double majors in the same school or college must complete all requirements for both majors and will receive one bachelor's degree when they graduate. For business students a second major in a liberal arts program fits well with the general requirements and/or free electives of a business program. It is also possible to complete two majors in two different schools or colleges and graduate with two bachelor's degrees. Normally completing the graduation requirements for two degrees takes at least one full additional year. Choosing a second major that has a great deal of curricular overlap with the first major can minimize the extra time.

I would not advocate a double undergraduate degree. The additional year you would spend to fulfill the requirements for the second degree could be used to substantially complete or in some cases complete a master's degree. A master's degree would probably be more useful than a second bachelor's degree.

A minor can offer you most of the benefits of a second major while requiring less additional course work. A typical minor might require about 12 semester units (18 quarter units) of course work. The minor can be used to strengthen your preparation in an area related to your major (e.g., computer applications, economics, accounting) or to gain breadth in a completely unrelated area (e.g., music, philosophy, creative writing).

Registration. The process of registering for your courses is extremely important. Through the registration process, you can ensure that you get the courses you need, the best instructors, and a good schedule. Not getting the courses you need can impede your progress, particularly in cases where you need the courses as prerequisites for future courses. Having the best available instructors can have a major impact on your academic success. And having a good schedule can ensure that you have adequate time for studying and other commitments such as outside work.

You will generally receive a priority for registration based on an ordering system established by your registrar's office. For example, the ordering system might have seniors registering first followed by, juniors, sophomores, and then first year students. If you have a low priority within your assigned group it may be difficult to get classes of your choice. You may be able to do something about it. Prior to registration meet with your academic adviser to verify that your priority is correct. Find out if any courses are being "saved" for your group to ensure you can complete prerequisites on time, and ask for registration tips to make the most of your registration window. Most importantly, register as soon as you are allowed. Far too many students register late because they were "too busy."

Leave of Absence/Withdrawal Policy. If you decide to leave the university, either for a temporary period or permanently, be sure to follow proper procedures. It is generally easy to gain approval for a leave of absence for purposes such as academic opportunities, study or travel abroad, field study, medical problems, financial reasons, or employment related to your educational goals. Even if you think you want to leave permanently, don't "burn your bridges." Your situation may change, and you may want to return at some point in the future.

Course Substitutes. Although the business course requirements may seem very rigid to you, some universities have a mechanism for substituting one business requirement for another. For example, you may want to explore the possibility of an *independent study* with a professor rather than taking a specific requirement. Generally, such substitutions can be made if you can gain the necessary approvals.

Overload Policy. Do you know the maximum number of units you can attempt in any one term? If you want to exceed that number, your university probably has an approval procedure established. And if your GPA is high, approval will probably be granted.

Credit for Courses at Other Institutions. You may want to take a course at a community college or other four-year institution during the summer. Before you do so, be sure to check out your university's transfer policy. Normally a grade of "C" or higher is required and only the units transfer, not the grade. Most likely, you must gain written approval in advance if you expect to receive transfer credit when you return.

Student Rights

There are regulations, policies, and procedures in the area of *student rights*. Your university probably has a *statement of student rights*. For example, my university publishes a student handbook that contains student life policies and procedures. You should be able to find references to the following:

1. You have a right to **receive advisement** about your academic program, your career goals, and university policies and procedures.

2. In the classroom, you have the right to **express your views, receive instruction**, and **be graded fairly**.

3. You have a right to **form and participate in clubs and organizations.**

4. You have the right to **publish or broadcast your opinions or concerns** to the campus community as long as they follow the rules of responsible journalism.

Check to see if your university or college has a similar statement of student rights.

> *Make sure you know what your rights are!*

We will discuss rights of students in three categories:

1) petitions

2) grievances

3) privacy of student records

Petitions. In the previous sections, we have given examples of the many rules, regulations, policies, and procedures which are part of the educational system in which you operate. However, as the old saying goes: "Every rule is made to be broken." If you find yourself constrained by a rule or regulation in a way that just doesn't make sense to you, you do have recourse. Every university has a procedure for *petition for waiver of regulations*. You may find a statement in your student handbook or university catalog that states:

> *Students who believe that extenuating circumstances might justify the waiver of a particular regulation or requirement may file a petition at their major department according to established procedures, for consideration by a faculty committee.*

If you cannot find a reference for a petition it is always a good idea to start with your major department office. The particular approval process can vary depending on the "seriousness" of the request to waive the rules. Suffice to say, if the necessary signatures can be obtained, anything is possible.

Student Grievances. Grievances are formal complaints by students against the university. The complaint might be about a specific instructor or administrator. Grievances generally involve an allegation by a student of unauthorized or unjustified actions that adversely affect the student's status, rights, or privileges, including but not limited to actions based on race, color, religion, sex, sexual orientation, national origin, age, handicap, or veteran status.

You should check on your university's student grievance policy. Generally, such policies outline specific processes for addressing student grievances. The student grievance process usually involves five steps. At the first step, the student is required to attempt to resolve the grievance informally with the faculty member. If this is not satisfactory, the student is required to next seek the help of the department chair in resolving the grievance informally. The next level is to file a formal written grievance with the department chair who may appoint a department level committee to make a recommendation. The fourth level is the school dean who may appoint a school-wide committee to make a recommendation, and the fifth level involves university arbitration with the Provost's Office, the Student Affairs Office, or a university student grievance committee.

Privacy of Student Records. Your university maintains various types of records about you including academic records, financial aid records, health center records, and employment records. The Federal Educational Rights and Privacy Act (FERPA) is a federal law designed to protect the privacy of your educational records. The following are your rights regarding these records:

1. You have the right to inspect and review all of your educational records maintained by the university.

2. You have the right to request that the university correct records you believe to be inaccurate or misleading.

3. Generally, the university must have written permission from you before releasing any information from your records. (Note: The law does

permit the university to disclose your records, without your consent, to certain parties.)

6.5 Student Conduct and Ethics

Along with rights come certain responsibilities. Your university has a code of conduct that delineates actions on your part which can result in disciplinary action. As an example, the following is a list of actions that warrant disciplinary action.

- Cheating or plagiarism in connection with an academic program at a campus

- Forgery, alteration, or misuse of campus documents, records, or identification or knowingly furnishing false information to a campus

- Misrepresentation of oneself or of an organization to be an agent of a campus

- Obstruction or disruption, on or off campus property, of the campus educational process, administrative process, or other campus function

- Physical abuse, on or off campus property, of the person or property of any member of the campus community or of members of his or her family or the threat of such physical abuse.

- Theft of, or non-accidental damage to, campus property, or property in the possession of, or owned by, a member of the campus community.

- Unauthorized entry into, unauthorized use, or misuse of campus property.

- On campus property, the sale or knowing possession of dangerous drugs, restricted dangerous drugs, or narcotics.

- Knowing possession or use of explosives, dangerous chemicals, or deadly weapons on campus property or at a campus function without prior authorization of the campus president.

- Engaging in lewd, indecent, or obscene behavior on campus property or at a campus function.

- Abusive behavior directed toward, or hazing of, a member of the campus community

- Violation of any order of a campus president or chancellor

- Soliciting or assisting another to do any act that would subject a student to expulsion, suspension or probation pursuant to this section.

All of the above behaviors can bring about disciplinary sanctions including assignment of a failing grade in a course, probation, suspension, and dismissal. Many of these acts are also crimes that can result in criminal prosecution in addition to university discipline.

Of these actions, the one that occurs most often is academic dishonesty. Because of its importance, it will be discussed in the next section.

Academic Honesty

During your business study, you will address the topic of ethics. *Ethics* is the study of what is right and what is wrong.

Ethics is a difficult subject because it is not always clear whether a certain behavior is ethical or unethical. Often business professionals face *dilemmas*—problems in which there are only two solutions, neither of which is satisfactory. Often we are faced with making the "least" unethical choice.

As a student, you will also face ethical dilemmas. Consider the following examples:

- You inadvertently saw several of the problems on an upcoming exam when you visited your professor in her office.

- Your professor incorrectly totaled the points on your midterm giving you a 78 when you really only scored 58.

- A friend has been sick and asks you whether he can copy your homework that is due in a few hours.

- You have a lousy professor who gives you a student opinion survey at the end of the course to evaluate his teaching and asks you to complete it and insert it in your final exam.

- Your professor has announced that his office hours are MW 10 a.m. - 12 noon. You have gone to his office during this time interval on four occasions and he has not been there.

- The data from your laboratory experiment doesn't make any sense at all. Your lab partner brings you a lab report from last term and suggests that you just use the data from that report.

- You are invited to be part of a group of students to meet with the chair of the AACSB visiting team. An administrator asks you not to say anything negative about the business program.

- You notice two students in your class exchange their test papers during the final exam.

What would you do in each of these situations? As you can see, in some cases, it is very easy to decide what's right. In other cases, it is much more difficult.

There are, however, some areas of academic honesty for which there is no confusion over right and wrong. These include cheating, fabrication, facilitating academic dishonesty, and plagiarism.

Cheating. *Cheating* is intentionally using or attempting to use unauthorized materials, information or study aids in any academic exercise. Specific examples of cheating are:

- **Receiving or knowingly supplying unauthorized information during an examination.**

- **Using unauthorized material/sources during an examination.**

- **Changing an answer after work has been graded, and presenting it as improperly graded.**

- **Taking an examination for another student or having another student take an examination for you.**

- **Forging or altering registration or grade documents**.

Fabrication. *Fabrication* is the intentional and unauthorized falsification or invention of any information or citation in an academic exercise.

Facilitating Academic Dishonesty. *Facilitating academic dishonesty* is intentionally or knowingly helping or attempting to help another to commit an act of academic dishonesty.

Plagiarism. *Plagiarism* is intentionally or knowingly representing the works or ideas of another as one's own in any academic exercise. The most extreme forms of plagiarism are the use of a paper written by another person or obtained from a commercial source or the use of passages copied word for word without acknowledgment.

6.6 Graduate Study in Business

Most of our discussion to this point has been directed at assisting you with the completion of your bachelor's degree. Upon completion of your undergraduate work, you will have a variety of options for what to do next. You can go to work in business, industry, or government, or you can continue your education by seeking a graduate degree. The graduate degree could be in business or in other areas such as law, medicine or liberal arts. Each of these opportunities for continuing your education will be briefly discussed in the following sections.

Benefits of Graduate Study in Business

Continuing your studies in a MS, MBA or Ph.D degree program will be an invaluable investment in yourself and in your future, regardless of what you plan to do professionally. The additional years you devote to graduate study can pay off again and again throughout your entire career in the following ways:

- You will gain self-esteem and self-confidence.

- You will broaden your career choices and open doors to more challenging jobs—both in academe and in business and industry.

- You will increase your potential earnings over your lifetime.

- You will gain increased prestige and others will accord you more respect.

Advanced Degrees in Business

MS Degree

The Master of Science degree in business is normally pursued immediately following the award of the business bachelor's degree. The M.S. allows you to specialize in a business discipline. Most programs are one to two years in length. A business undergraduate degree is normally required for admission.

The following list identifies a few of the M.S. programs you can find at business schools.

- The Master of Science in Accountancy program can provide you with a broad-based business education, equipping you with the necessary technical knowledge, communication skills, and critical thinking abilities expected by employers and required of future leaders and accounting professionals.

- The Master of Science degree in Management Information Systems can teach you in-depth skills that will enable you to develop and manage computer-based information systems.

- The Masters of Science in Finance can provide you with advanced education in financial theory and management. Programs normally emphasize applied research and modeling as well as the global and regulatory dimensions of finance.

- The Master of Science in Project Management degree program can offer a set of core courses that provide a foundation in the fundamentals of management analysis and strategy.

MBA Degree

MBA programs expose students to a common body of knowledge in basic areas including accounting, economics, organizational behavior, statistics and quantitative methods, finance, marketing, operations and policy. Students usually select more concentrated study or track in one or more elective areas.

Many schools offer joint degree programs, so students can earn an MBA and a law degree or an MBA and an engineering degree or an MBA and a Science degree. In the past, traditional MBA applicants were non-business students. However this trend has changed and many MBA programs encourage and accept students who have completed an undergraduate business bachelor's program. Most MBA programs have an accelerated version of the MBA for the undergraduate business degree student. The accelerated program normally can be finished in one year and opportunities for employment are equal to other MBA graduates. Those with more than six years of business experience might want to consider an executive MBA program. Usually held on weekends and lasting for 18 months or so, these intensive programs hold special appeal for experienced managers.

Regardless of your academic background, quality MBA programs prefer a student to have a minimum of three years of work experience before you apply for admission. Completing your MBA degree can take from one year of full-time study to two years depending on your qualifications, choice of program, and decision to be part-time or full time.

Ph.D. Degree

The Doctor of Philosophy (Ph.D.) degree is the highest educational degree in business. It generally takes four or five years of full-time study beyond the bachelor's degree. Typically, a Ph.D. program consists of about two years of course work culminating in comprehensive examinations (*comps*) covering your areas of specialty. After you pass the *comps*, you will work full-time on a major research project, which becomes your Ph.D. dissertation. Normally, you would apply for admission to a Ph.D. program following completion of your Masters degree. Most business students will move on to another institution for the Ph.D. This is a broadening experience and it will extend your academic horizons.

You can be admitted directly into the Ph.D. program upon completion of your bachelors degree. In some cases you simply "pick up" a masters degree along the way with little or no additional work. At other places, you may be required to take a special exam or complete a masters thesis to get the masters degree. At still other places, you can elect to skip the master's degree completely.

The Ph.D. degree can prepare you for a career either in business or industry or academe. A career as a business professor can provide special rewards. If you would like to know more about these rewards ask your professor or I suggest that you read *An Academic Career: It Could Be For You.* [3]

Full-time or Part-time?

It is possible to work full-time in industry and pursue graduate study in business on a part-time basis. This is the way many students obtain their MBA degrees. But it is much more difficult, if not impossible, to complete a Ph.D. degree on a part-time basis. Whether earning an MBA or a Ph.D., I certainly advise you to consider full-time graduate study if you can arrange it. Many of the benefits of graduate education come from being fully immersed in the academic environment such as the concentrated study in your area of specialty; the engaging dialogue with faculty and other graduate students; and the advantage of carrying out research under the close supervision of a faculty adviser.

There are some benefits to working full-time in industry for a period of time after you receive your bachelors degree and then returning to full-time graduate study. You will have a break from school. You will have the opportunity to at least start paying off incurred debts. You have the opportunity to apply what you have learned. There is, however, a potential problem with working too long in industry. You may get used to a full-time salary, making it difficult to return to the more modest student life. Of course, this depends on you and your commitment to your education.

How Will You Support Yourself?

Graduate study is different from undergraduate study in that there is a good chance you will be paid to do it. Any business graduate who has the potential to get a Ph.D. should have a good chance of lining up adequate financial support for full-time graduate study. There are three kinds of financial support for graduate study: fellowships, teaching assistantships, and research assistantships. All three usually cover tuition and fees and provide a stipend for living expenses. Although fellowships and assistantships provide you much less money than full-time industrial positions, they provide adequate support so that you can devote full-time to getting your degree in the least possible time.

6.7 Role of Research

Business faculty are expected to perform in three primary categories: 1) teaching; 2) research; and 3) service. Your interaction with professors is mostly through their teaching role. However, most faculty members are also extensively involved in research. Research involves creating and organizing new knowledge and disseminating that knowledge through publications in scholarly journals and presentations at academic and professional conferences.

The balance between teaching, research, and service varies from one university to the next, depending on the characteristics of the institution. At one end are the *research universities*, which place a strong emphasis on graduate education and research. Teaching loads at these institutions are relatively light—usually one or two courses a term. At the other end of the spectrum are primarily undergraduate universities, which emphasize teaching. At these institutions, the teaching requirement may be heavier—usually three or four courses a term. Some research is expected, but much less than at research institutions.

There are opportunities for undergraduate students to work on research projects. However, the primary effect of a college's research program on you is in the way it impacts your professors—both positively and negatively. The positive value of research is that it contributes to the professional development of the faculty. Professors who are working on the frontiers of knowledge in their fields of specialty are likely to be very up-to-date and to be enthusiastic about their work. On the negative side, the demands of seeking funding for research projects and conducting an active research program can leave professors with reduced time and energy to focus on the education of undergraduate students.

6.8 Graduate Study Opportunities Are Not Limited to Business

The undergraduate business degree is good preparation for whatever you would like to pursue. Business study is particularly good preparation for graduate study in fields such as law, medicine, and some liberal arts programs. Each of these opportunities is discussed briefly in the following sections.

Law

There are no specific undergraduate course requirements for law school, nor is there a specific pre law curriculum. Although many pre-law students major in political science, any major including business is acceptable.

Admission to one of the 176 American Bar Association (ABA) accredited law schools in the U.S. is based on undergraduate transcripts, letters of recommendation, and scores on the Law School Aptitude Test (LSAT). Law school admissions officers are also increasing favoring applicants with work experience and maturity.

If you are interested in law school, you should concentrate your elective courses in history, economics, political science, and logic. Strong reading, writing, and oral communication skills are critical. Any opportunities you have to gain familiarity with legal terminology and the judicial process will be beneficial in law school. Most universities have a pre-law advisor. I would recommend you visit with this person as soon as possible in order to gain the best insight to the opportunities offered by your institution for the pre-law student.

Medicine

Business study can be excellent preparation for medical school. The National Summary of the 1997 entering class of medical students states that of the 15,532 students accepted into the nation's medical schools, 172 (1.1 percent) received their undergraduate degree in business [4]. The acceptance rate for business graduates who applied (31 percent) is comparable to the acceptance rate of all applicants (36 percent).

It is no accident that business graduates can compete on an equal level with other medical school applicants. The logical thinking and problem solving skills developed through business study have a direct carry-over to the diagnostic skills practiced by physicians. Doctors can also benefit from a strong business background and once you start medical school is it very unlikely you will have time to take any business courses. The combination of business and medicine can lead to a very successful career as a doctor. After all, the field of medicine is a business.

Business graduates have another benefit over the more traditional pre-med majors such as biology, chemistry, and health science. Business offers students an excellent "fall-back" career option if they are either unable to gain admission to medical school or lose interest in a medical career.

Admission to medical school is based on undergraduate grades, scores on the Medical Careers Aptitude Test (MCAT), letters of recommendation, a personal statement, and a personal interview. Work experience is increasingly considered as a positive factor. The MCAT is given twice each year and contains four sections: 1) verbal reasoning; 2) physical sciences; 3) writing sample; and 4) biological sciences.

Preparation for the MCAT and for admission to medical school should be considered as early as possible in your undergraduate program. Wise and judicious use of your free electives will certainly enhance your probability of success. Your preparation should include two courses in general chemistry with labs, two courses in organic chemistry with labs, two courses in general biology with labs, and two courses in physics with labs. Like all opportunities in life, planning will help you to achieve your objectives. I recommend you seek out the pre-med advisor at your institution for guidance.

Liberal Arts

Business education can be used to gain admissions into graduate programs in liberal arts. Earlier in this chapter we discussed the AACSB accreditation standards, and one of the basic standards of accreditation states that the business program curriculum should consist of an equal mix of business and non-business courses. You will be required to take a number of liberal arts courses in order to complete your degree and you may even declare a second major or a minor in a liberal arts program. Your undergraduate program will include courses in such as areas as economics, history, philosophy, theology, sociology, psychology, anthropology, political science, and English. You may decide to continue your education in one these fields. Business-related fields of study in liberal arts include but are not limited to economics, mathematics, psychology, and communications.

Summary

Understanding the education system of which you are a part will better prepare you to make that system work for you. We described how the business school or college fits into the overall organization of the university.

We described the importance and the depth of the business accreditation process as administered by the International Association for Management Education (AACSB). Business programs are evaluated in the areas of mission, faculty, curriculum, instruction, students, and intellectual contributions. To be accredited, a business program must meet high standards of quality in each of these areas.

We also discussed the important area of academic advising including curricular advising and career advising. Ways were outlined in which you can ensure that you receive quality academic advising regardless of the advising system in place at your institution.

Next, we described various academic regulations, policies, and procedures with which you need to be familiar. Through an understanding of these regulations, policies, and procedures, you can ensure that the system works for you and not against you. We also discussed the important area of student rights including the right to petition, the right to file grievances, and the right to privacy of records.

Along with these rights goes responsibility. We discussed the responsibility of students to conduct themselves ethically and honestly.

Finally, we discussed opportunities to continue your education beyond the bachelors degree. Graduate study in business can lead you to the Masters in Business Administration, the MBA, and the Ph.D. degrees. Opportunities to seek post-graduate education in other professional fields including law and medicine as well as liberal arts were also presented.

References

1. The AACSB WEBSITE, *http://www.aacsb.edu/opt1.html*, December 4, 1997.

2. *Achieving Quality and Improvement through Self-Evaluation and Peer Review, Standards for Accreditation Business and Accounting Handbook,* Revised April 12,1994. (Available from AACSB, 600 Emerson Road, Suite 300. St Louis MO 63141-6762)

3. Landis, R.B., "An Academic Career: It Could Be For You," *Engineering Education,* July/August 1989. (Available from American Society for Engineering Education, Washington, D.C.)

4. "AAMC Section For Student Services Admission Action Summary," National Summary 1997 Entering Class, Association of American

Medical Colleges, 2450 N Street, NW, Washington, D.C. 20037-1129, 1993.

Exercises

1. Find out the names of the people in the following positions:

    a)   The chair or head of your business department.

    b)   The dean of your business college.

    c)   The provost or vice president for academic affairs.

    d)   The president or chancellor of your university.

2. Find out where you will learn the following computer skills in your curriculum:

    a. Word-processing

    b. Spread sheets

    c. Database management systems

    d. Data acquisition

3. Lay out a term-by-term plan for the courses you will take to meet all of the requirements for your business degree. Review this plan with your academic adviser and revise it based on the feedback you receive.

4. Research the academic advising system in place at your institution. Write a one-page description of that advising system including your critique of how well it is working for you.

5. Does your institution publish a *Student Handbook*? *A Statement of Student Rights? A Student Code of Conduct?* Obtain copies and read them thoroughly.

6. Find out your university's specific regulations regarding the following academic issues:

    a. Taking Courses *Pass/Fail or Credit/No Credit*

    b. Drop/Add Policy

    c. Repeat Grade Policy

    d. Credit by Examination

    e. Probation

    f. Dismissal

   g. Dean's List

   h. Honors at graduation

7. After you have completed 100 units, your overall GPA is 2.4. During the next term you take 16 units and achieve a 3.4 GPA for the term. What is your overall GPA then? If your overall GPA was 3.4 after 100 units and you take 16 units and make a 2.4 GPA for the term, what is your overall GPA then? What is the *moral* of this exercise?

8. Write a brief opinion as to how you would handle the ethical dilemma of observing a friend cheating on homework versus observing the same friend cheating on an exam.

9. Find out how you go about changing your business major. Are some majors more difficult to get into than others are? Which major is the most difficult to get into?

10. Investigate the graduate programs available at your institution. Which programs offer masters degrees? Which programs offer Ph.D. degrees? Look into the admissions standards (e.g., GPA, Graduate Record Examination scores, etc.) for graduate study in your major.